Glowing Comments from Leaders Endorsing *Just Ask!*...

"*Just Ask!* is the best book I've ever read on asking clear, compassionate and compelling questions in opening up genuine human interactions! This very readable illustrated book gives an invaluable tool for both your professional and personal life."

—**Stephen R. Covey**
Author of *The 7 Habits of Highly Effective People* and
The 8th Habit: From Effectiveness to Greatness

"Bill's knowledge, heart, and passion is to positively impact the lives of every person he comes in contact with, either in person, on the phone, through an email, in a seminar, or through his writings. I highly recommend *Just Ask!* as an excellent read for improving your chances of success in whatever you choose to do."

—**W. Kent Lutz**
Director, Goering Center for Family & Private Business,
Adjunct Professor, Entrepreneurship/Finance,
College of Business, University of Cincinnati

"The skills in *Just Ask!* are endless. As you apply these tools, your success will be even more effective."

—**Nancy Lauterbach**
Founder and Former President, FIVE STAR Speakers &
Trainers, International Association of Speakers Bureaus

"McGrane is on target—a well-researched challenge is half-solved. Is there any reason not to read this book?"

—Gregg Fraley
Creativity and Innovation Expert,
Author of *Jack's Notebook*

"One of the most powerful skills and tools that one can use to build rapport, gain intimacy, and create desired outcomes relationally, vocationally, and every other way is the art of asking questions. One of the most effective and brilliant masters of this tool is Bill McGrane III, a man I consider both a mentor and a friend.

"What you hold in your hand is a life-long resource of some of his greatest insights and strategies for discovering, developing, and deploying this incredible skill and tool. Take your time as you read through this and, then, for every insight you gain, ground it in practice in your life. What will make the difference is doing what you read in these pages."

—Mark J. Chironna, MA, PhD
Creating Your World LLC

"This book takes the principle of 'ask and you shall receive' to new dimensions. In his down-to-earth manner, Bill walks you, step by step, through the questioning process so you can BE more, DO more, and HAVE more!"

—Brent Dearing
Founder and President, Wealth Transfer Int'l

"This book provides you the tools to be more successful and persuasive. Mastering the skills of asking questions opens doors you can only imagine."

—Gary D. Green
CEO, Strategic Franchising Systems, Inc.

"How will this book change your life? I'm so glad you asked! Bill McGrane shows you how to use skillful questioning to improve your relationships, achieve more goals, build better rapport, and take your business to the next level!"

—**Tamara Lowe**
Co-Founder and Executive Vice President,
Get Motivated Seminars, Inc.

"Ask the question that gives the perfect end result. Incorporating and using this process has helped me to expand and master this craft and the art of asking questions.

"Exploring and discovering the deeper levels of the art of asking questions with Bill has been and continues to be a new frontier of adventure in self-discovery and continuing success with no limits in sight.

"This is the ultimate power tool that puts me in authority, gives me dominion over renewing my thinking, forms empowering beliefs, opens the door of expectations, determines my attitude, elevates my emotions, and is expressed in my behaviors giving me the desired end result most of the time…. That's what I call FUN!

"Thank you, Bill, with all my heart; I'm now living the dream…."

—**Kirk Metz**
Million Dollar Earner, Isagenix International

"*Just Ask!* is phenomenal! On our first date over the phone, I interviewed my wife for four hours asking question after question. I also use the skills for screening potential employees and my business has soared. *Just Ask!* really works!"

—**Michael Shober**
President, Shober Training & Development, Inc.

"Asking the right questions is essential to helping people heal. Bill's book gives you the tools and the skills to help others by asking the best questions."

—Dr. Bill King Chiropractor

Just Ask!

Success Can
Be as Simple as
Asking
the Right
Questions

Bill McGrane III

A *Possibility Press* Book

Just Ask!

Bill McGrane III

Copyright © 2008 by Bill McGrane III
ISBN 978-0-938716-65-5
Cover Photo by Tim O'Brien

1   2   3   4   5   6   7   8   9   10

Published by
Possibility Press
PossibilityPress.com

Manufactured in the United States of America

Dedication

To my father, William J. McGrane, Jr., who shared everything he had—challenging me to live up to my potential. You taught me the skills of the art of asking questions.

Acknowledgment

Thank you, Walter Cronkite, for setting a standard of excellence in asking questions. When asked how he selected interview guests, Walter said, "It's easy to find people willing to talk about their successes. I find my audience listens most to those people willing to talk about their challenges and how they have overcome them."

Thank you, God, for my challenges and everyone who has had a hand in my life. I often ask people, "Who has made the greatest impact on your life?" As for me, I am grateful to the Lord for giving me the abilities I have.

Thank you, Dean McGrane, my mother, who taught me the caring side of life.

Thank you, Joan and Kit, my sisters, and Bob, my brother, and other relatives. You've all helped me live a life open to more possibilities.

Thank you, Linda, my wife and partner, and our four children, Jay, Heidi, Laura, and John for your love and support.

I appreciate the thousands of clients and organizations with whom I've been privileged to share the many life-changing principles I've learned over the years.

Many special thanks to my editor and publisher. Without your dedication and personal interest in me and my mission, this book would not be what it is or even exist.

Contents

Chapter One

The Way You Ask a Question Affects the Response!

Are your communication skills getting you the results you want? Would you like to have some new ways to empower your ability to persuade? If you could improve one aspect of your communications skills, what would it be? Could asking questions and listening more skillfully make a difference for you?

The benefits of asking questions are endless. By first asking the best questions of yourself you can stay focused on the most important things. They'll help you get your mind thinking in the right direction, remove obstacles to your success, stop you from making self-defeating choices, and empower you to receive creative answers to what's vital in your life.

Asking questions of others enables you to learn more about them—how they think, feel, view life, and what they aspire to. You'll be better able to share what you have to offer based on what they need. You'll have the resources to more effectively handle objections and resolve and dissipate conflict.

Picture this: You walk into a department store, and while you're making your way through the specialty kitchen section of the appliance area, you hear an older woman yelling. As you turn toward the customer service counter, where people can pay their local utility bills, you hear the woman shouting, "How could my electric bill be so high? You've got to be kidding!" From the tone of her voice, you know immediately that an explosion is about to occur.

Across the aisle, you sit down in a lounge chair and act like a quiet little mouse. You're curious to listen and see how this situation unfolds. You notice that the employees seem to suddenly become very busy with all kinds of activities except, that is, assisting this woman. They've obviously decided to ignore her and act as if nothing is happening. Meanwhile, the older woman, who's getting more agitated by the minute, is quickly walking around and around a nearby table, shouting in disbelief about her utility bill. Everyone is well aware of what's going on, but no one's doing anything to help. Then a magic moment occurs— someone with the skill to resolve the issue is about to step in.

If you were faced with this situation, what would *you* do? What would be the first thing you'd say? Might it be appropriate to ask a question?

Observing all of this is a woman in the appliance area; she's demonstrating a coffee machine and giving away free samples. As the older woman came around the table again, she noticed the coffee lady who then gently asked her, "Would you like a cup of coffee?" Immediately, the older woman went from showing extreme pain to relative calmness—the result of the power of a question! It was as if the coffee lady knew exactly what to ask to defuse a hostile situation, releasing the pressure and tension. She asked the right question and won the day!

The older woman said, "Yes," and the coffee lady continued having the conversation, adding the power of touch. As she put her hand on the older woman's arm she said, "Let's talk about this for a minute. Do you like cream in your coffee?" The coffee lady's question reframed the situation, putting it in a different light, and the older woman totally calmed down. You could actually feel the tension and pressure being released. It seemed like a miracle as everyone in the room breathed a silent sigh of relief.

By this time the store manager had come into the picture to help, even though the situation had nothing to do with him. The challenge was a utility bill that the older woman believed was incorrect. Like many people, she didn't have the skill to ask the appropriate questions. She felt there was only one way to deal with the situation—anger and yelling.

Consider this: You're sitting in your home or office trying to figure out your next step. You may be frustrated because you've done this many times and lots of things are going through your mind, confusing you even more. You ask yourself, "Do I focus on this project, make this call, or handle this family issue?"

In sorting out your next step, you probably did one of two things: You either continued coming up with more things to add to your to-do list, continuing to keep yourself in a loop of inaction or, if you knew the steps to get you off the perpetual treadmill, you could move from inaction to inspired accomplishment.

Here's another example: You're talking with a prospective client. You think you've done your homework and anticipate they'll do business with you. As you get into your presentation, you notice they're not responding the way you thought they would. All of a sudden, they ask you some questions you either don't know the answers to or have no clue about what to do next. You try to compose yourself to come up with the best thing to say. Unfortunately, their response to what you do say next indicates they're just as confused as you are. You have no idea what to say or do now to fix the situation so you can get your presentation back on track toward making the sale or getting the agreement you're looking for.

On a personal level, have you ever found yourself in a situation praying, "Oh God, please show me a way out of this conversation"? The love of your life wants your feedback on how you're going to resolve an issue with a family member. What you're hearing tells you this conversation is going down the path of no return. The two of you have argued about this before. You hate conflict so, as usual, you try to scurry around the topic. However, you're feeling cornered and see no way out.

You've got to do something! In your mind you begin seeing your pattern of avoidance repeating itself over and over again whenever you come to a sticky point where uncomfortable action is required. You desperately try to think of a way out. Instead, your mind locks up with fear. You're sure the look on your face shows you're confused, which could be taken as guilt even though you did nothing wrong. You're so stressed out you even admit to things you never did, wondering, "How can I avoid getting into a situation like this again?"

If you can relate to any of these scenarios the good news is you're not alone. The even better news is there's a simple and effective way through these situations—by asking questions—which is what this book is all about. It gives you the tools to handle these and thousands of other situations that arise, as well as initiating and creating the results you want, enabling you to live more successfully.

Now take the following quiz to identify your skill in asking questions and your attitude toward it:

1. Do I like asking questions? ___Yes ___No

2. Do I feel comfortable asking
   questions? ___Yes ___No

3. Am I able to construct interesting
   questions? ___Yes ___No

4. Do I know what questions to ask? ___Yes ___No

5. Am I courageous in asking
   questions? ___Yes ___No

6. Am I interested enough in others to
   ask questions of them?   ___Yes ___No

7. Do I realize the questions I ask
   affect the quality of my life and
   that of those around me?   ___Yes ___No

8. When people talk to me, do I listen
   and remember what they say?   ___Yes ___No

9. Do others consider me a great
   conversationalist because I
   listen well?   ___Yes ___No

10. Am I skillful enough to ask questions
    so I can get to the bottom of things?   ___Yes ___No

11. Do I find people have an easy
    time answering my questions?   ___Yes ___No

12. Do I ask questions rather than
    making statements?   ___Yes ___No

13. Do I find myself persuading others
    more than they persuade me?   ___Yes ___No

14. Do I ask questions instead of just
    talking about myself?   ___Yes ___No

15. Do I find it easy to start a conver-
    sation?   ___Yes ___No

16. Do I find it easy to keep a conver-
    sation going?   ___Yes ___No

17. Do I find it easy to end a conver-
    sation?   ___Yes ___No

18. Do I ask questions without being
    afraid of the answer I may get back?   ___Yes ___No

19. Do I ask enough questions of enough
    people?   ___Yes ___No

20. Do I understand that I could increase
    my income by asking the right
    questions?   ___Yes ___No

Count your yes answers and put the total here: ____

What Your Answers Mean

- 0-6 yeses: You're at the beginning stages of asking questions. This book will definitely help you be a more effective communicator.

- 7-13 yeses: You see the value of asking questions. You'll gain the tools to be more effective in asking questions to win more.

- 14-20 yeses: Mean you have developed many keys in the art of asking skills. Keep reading and take your skills to a whole new level.

A Tool to Success in Building Better Relationships

Words are powerful; they create feelings! Choose and use them well. The words you choose have the power to literally change lives—including yours. When we think positive thoughts and use positive words, things go more smoothly. Words affect people. For example, advertising would be meaningless if words didn't impact people!

Dr. David Hawkins tells us words have different frequencies. Words like thank you, love, and gratitude help raise the frequency of the thoughts, feelings, and interactions of both parties.

Can you feel how "Let's do it" has a higher frequency than "Do it"? Low frequency words will, of course, lower the feelings in and the outcomes for both parties. Can you feel the difference in your body as you say, "Let's do it" vs. "Do it"? The *perceived* meaning of your communications largely determines the outcomes you get.

When you ask questions, you give people an opportunity to respond, encouraging them to use their personal power with dignity. How you feel about yourself at the time you're asking a question will determine how you use questions. You can always tell your level of self-esteem by the questions you ask or don't ask.

Words are powerful; they create feelings! Choose and use them well.

Questions tell others you care enough about them to take the time to learn more about them, what they're feeling, what they need. You can shine a light of caring and love over them by asking questions. When your self-esteem is healthy, you'll find yourself using questions to uplift and encourage the people around you. Then watch what happens! People will come alive and love you for making it happen.

There's definitely an art to asking questions—of yourself as well as others. You can ask yourself appropriate, effective questions to help you get the outcomes you want in your personal and professional relationships. The questions you ask yourself and how effectively you answer them determines the degree to which you'll be able to ask effective questions of others.

My father, William J. McGrane, Jr., was a master teacher. His life was filled with his own emotional pain and problematic self-esteem, and because of what he observed and experienced he constantly asked himself two questions: "Why do I and others hurt so much, and what can be done about it?" As a result, he embarked on a life-long quest researching self-esteem, beginning when he was a senior in high school. Dad knew there had to be an answer to what was causing him so much pain.

In college, he learned that words had power and soon became a wordsmith. He began abusing their power, using them inappropriately—increasingly intimidating those around him. He'd feel powerful for a moment, yet his pain would only increase, driving him to search for a way to relieve it.

When I was a kid, my dad didn't have the skill of asking questions. Even though things looked great on the outside, he was still searching for the reason he hurt so much on the inside. As a result of his lack of skill, I was one of the recipients of his sharp tongue as he "sliced and diced" me with his words.

In 1967, he attended a personal development program and discovered one of the missing pieces to his pain puzzle—he talked too much! He then consciously started asking questions, figuring it was one way he could say something yet be silent while listening to what others had to say. Dad immediately began receiving better outcomes, and his pain somewhat diminished. However, something was *still* missing, as much of his emotional pain still remained. He would still harm people's self-esteem with his stabbing, mean use of words. Dad continued researching self-esteem, determined to find the answer to the foundational question of his life: "Why do I and others hurt so much, and what can be done about it?"

In March 1976, Dad, my brother, Bob, and I attended a break-through-in-awareness program to help us move on from old, ineffective thinking and behavior. It was then that everything came together for my father. He finally discovered the last missing piece: "value judging" was causing his pain! He had been comparing his value to that of others. As it turns out, value judging is the only thing that can injure or destroy self-esteem. It was a dramatic epiphany and, ironically, it was his own personal pain that allowed him to recognize it. All of his schooling, reading, studying, attending seminars, listening to audio programs, and researching of self-esteem finally made sense. It had all come together.

Immediately, Dad's behavior began to change. He no longer used his wordsmithing skills to destroy or slice and dice people. He went from being like a roaring lion to a gentle fawn. I watched this process in awe as my father refined his skills and, accordingly, changed his behavior. He became a master role model and teacher of three things: self-esteem, asking questions, and external listening (listening to others).

Since Dad preached what he practiced, I was open to accepting and learning from him. He was a master resource to me, which now enables me to share this information with you. His greatest contribution to the world was sharing the results of his study on self-esteem.

Self-esteem is the respect you feel for yourself; it is a *feeling*. It has nothing to do with how much money you have or make, your reputation, the clothes you wear, where you live, or your zip code. It doesn't matter how you have focused your life, whether you have riches or nothing. Self-esteem is multifaceted. It's always fluctuating; it's always in process. It's intangible; however, it can be recognized in your behavior. Self-esteem is reflected in how you treat yourself and others.

It's important to understand the dynamics of self-esteem when you ask questions. When you have self-esteem, you can use it to support your ability in asking questions. You can honor people with questions to show interest and caring. However, if you base your life on self-image—an imitation, representation, or false front of what you'd like others to believe about you (a lack of self-esteem)—you're likely to be manipulative and exploitative of others as you pursue the outcomes you want!

If you conduct your life from a self-image perspective, you'll be self-centered in going for what you want, without regard for others. You'll be concerned only about yourself and unwilling to sincerely serve anyone. This thinking and its resulting behavior occurs throughout the world. History is full of the disastrous outcomes it has produced along the way.

For best results in relating with others, always use self-esteem-enhancing words while asking questions. This will help you obtain elegant, exquisite, and irresistible outcomes for everyone. When you integrate self-esteem with asking questions, you can use your skills to assist others in discovering the outcomes that can best serve them as well as you.

The Tree of Self-Image and Self-Esteem

The last gift my father left behind to grow, which pictorially reinforces the importance of self-esteem, is *The Tree of Self-Image and Self-Esteem*. Picture a tree where the left side is dead, bearing no leaves. This represents self-image behavior, which is based on comparison. The words on this side of *The Tree* are the result of living a self-image lifestyle, sadly creating self-hatred. Self-image tells you what you should, ought, or must be, do, and have. Have you ever been told you should or shouldn't do something? You should do this; you ought to do that; you must do thus and so! Can you feel the energy drain caused by those words? This hurts your self-esteem and shows up in your behavior as well as in the words with which you communicate.

Review the following words on the self-image (self-hatred), left side of *The Tree,* and recognize how you feel when you read them: emotional abuse, dependency, depression, gossip, crime, guilt, fear, shame, apathy, flattery, rejection, jealousy, labeling, emptiness, insecurity, addictions, and egocentricity. They all bring you to the roots of self-image behavior—value judging and comparison. We've all experienced these to varying degrees, along with the negative feelings they created.

I encourage you to, right now, begin releasing any feelings of self-image you may have. Especially be aware of when you are comparing yourself to others or labeling them—then let it go! Kirkigard said, "Once you label me you negate me." Realize that you are valuable and intelligent just the way you are. You are one of a kind—there is no one exactly like you.

No one person has all the answers. So, just as my dad did, start asking for *your* missing piece. It's acceptable and essential to ask questions of yourself. When we ask questions based on self-esteem, we uplift our own lives, as well as the lives of those with whom we come in contact.

Now picture the right side of *The Tree*. It's alive and well, flourishing with beautiful green leaves. The branches consist of these words: encouragement, peace of mind, fulfillment, affirming, patience, playful, health, joy, trust, purpose, integrity, creativity, acceptance, forgiveness, commitment, responsibility, and inner directed. All of them bring us to the roots of self-esteem (self-respect)—faith, hope, love, and TUA (Total Unconditional Acceptance). TUA is the cornerstone of McGrane Global Center's principles. The more TUA you give and experience in your life, the more you'll be able to apply the skills you'll be learning here. Your skill in asking questions is directly related to your ability to practice TUA.

Five Steps to Developing the Art of Asking Questions

You probably haven't given much thought to the idea that there's an art to asking questions. The prerequisite or *first step* in developing that art is to *ask questions with self-esteem*. To ask questions effectively you need self-esteem. You need to feel respect for yourself before you can give it to others. The more self-esteem you have, the more you are able to take your eyes off yourself and be totally present and focused on the person or people to whom you are speaking.

"So where do I begin?" you may ask.

The Tree

of Self-Image
(Self-Hatred)

- Emotional Abuse
- Dependency
- Depression
- Gossip
- Crime
- Guilt
- Fear
- Shame
- Apathy
- Flattery
- Rejection
- Jealousy
- Labeling
- Emptiness
- Insecurity
- Addictions
- Egocentricity

of Self-Esteem
(Self-Respect)

- Encouragement
- Peace of Mind
- Fulfillment
- Affirming
- Patience
- Playful
- Health
- Joy
- Trust
- Purpose
- Integrity
- Creativity
- Acceptance
- Forgiveness
- Commitment
- Responsibility
- Inner Directed

Value Judging & Comparison   Faith, Hope, Love, & T.U.A.

Since questions involve putting words together, what's the best way to do that with self-esteem? What words do you use during your self-talk? What words do you use when you're speaking to others? Are they positive or negative, affirming or putting down? Are you aware of the feelings your words are creating in yourself and others? Words are so powerful that their emotional impact can stay with us throughout our lives. And since self-esteem is a feeling, words affect our own self-esteem, as well as that of others.

As you express yourself, know that you can give others only what you yourself possess. If your self-talk and what you say to others is negative and demeaning, you injure your own self-esteem as well as that of others. However, when your self-talk is positive and affirming, you *boost* your self-esteem as well as theirs. What a great incentive to monitor and upgrade any self-talk and conversation with others that may be hindering your or their progress!

The *second step* in developing the art of asking questions is to *become aware of the impact your words have on yourself and others*. Notice the feelings you create within yourself with the words you use and recognize that what you say to others can impact them for a lifetime.

Can you recall the words significant people in your life have said to you—possibly your father, mother, brother, sister, teacher, mentor, manager, friend, or spouse? Even if you don't recall the person who said those words, nonetheless, the words are still with you! Has anyone ever used words in an attempt to put you down or make you feel inferior? How were those words expressed and how did you feel in response to them? What words were used by someone who loves you? What did he or she say and what feelings were created in you by those words? Relax and allow whatever comes up to emerge. Write it down. Did you come up with any comments or statements made to you, perhaps even years ago? If you did, then you appreciate the power of words, their impact on you, and how long they've stayed with you.

My third-grade teacher used to say, "Bill, never talk in front of people because they'll laugh at you." As a young boy, I slurred my Ss and Ts and needed to be taught how to speak. The problem, though, was that I interpreted her statement to mean, "Bill, shut up! Don't talk to people. They'll only laugh at you." The impact of those words caused me to remain quiet and shy for five years!

The ***third step*** in developing the art of asking questions is to *refine your skill of external listening*. Quiet the conversation you're having with yourself and focus on hearing what the other person is saying.

Now ask yourself these questions:

- Have you ever been at a meeting, seminar, or in a conversation and had no idea what was being said?

- Do you ever tune people out once you hear them say words that remind you of something unpleasant?

- Do you ever not listen to someone because you're thinking about what you're going to say when it's your turn to talk?

- Have you ever found yourself interrupting another to share your ideas, impressions, or opinions before that person finishes his or her comments?

- Is it typical for you to listen to people—in a token manner, not really hearing nor understanding what they're saying? Are you sometimes jolted into realizing this because you caught only the tail-end of a question they've just asked you and need to ask them to repeat it?

- Do you sometimes totally ignore people, including children, because you believe they'll never say anything of interest or importance to you?

If you answered yes to any of those questions, pay extra attention to this step. Listening is affected by selective exposure, selective retention, experiences, and perception—whether we're consciously aware of these factors or not. We listen through filters impacted by our levels of understanding, upbringing, culture, value system, social tendencies, education, relationships, and the list goes on. Research shows that most people are willing to listen to someone only as long as 80 percent of what's being said blends with their own beliefs.

To enhance your ability to ask questions, you need to *hear* what the person in front of you or on the phone is saying. Give your undivided attention to that person. Nothing can be going on inside of you. Quiet your internal dialogue or self-talk—what you're saying to yourself in your head—most of which originates at the subconscious level. You may never quiet all of your internal dialogue; however, it is possible to take charge of more of it.

Again, become more aware of your self-talk. Write it down and begin to recognize how it may be holding you back or moving you forward. Is it beneficial or detrimental to you? Take some quiet time and focus on yourself and your internal dialogue. It could be as simple as noticing your self-talk while driving to work. Are you putting yourself in a positive or negative frame of mind?

Reframe anything that's not serving you. For example, instead of saying to yourself, "I can't make it happen," say "I *can* make it happen." Be keenly aware of your internal dialogue and how it affects yourself and others. Take charge of it by noticing what you are saying to yourself, observing how it makes you feel, and fine-tuning as needed. Make a conscious effort to consider the idea you're thinking about in another way. This may include giving someone the benefit of the doubt—considering the circumstances that may have affected his or her behavior. (This'll help anyone who tends to have a victim mentality, which is disempowering.) Or it could be forgiving yourself for a mistake you've made and committing to avoid repeating it.

Until you take better charge of your thoughts and still your mind, it's impossible for you to focus on anyone else. Change your behavior by focusing on thinking about and working toward what you *do* want. When you do, you'll be free to focus on the person you're talking with. This takes not only self-discipline and an alert mind, but also staying mentally in the present moment. Don't think about the past or worry about the future—you'd only be focusing on what you don't want to happen. *Practice, practice, practice!* It's a fun, lifelong adventure.

When you're sincerely focused on someone else, you can listen, truly hear, and are more likely to comprehend what they're saying. You'll get a better sense of the feelings behind their words, and be able to communicate with more compassion and understanding. This will help you better identify where people actually are rather than projecting on them according to your own agenda of where you want them to be. As they share what's going on with them, you'll be able to pick up on their core criteria—what's most important to them. Knowing this, you can then create a "designer" question by using *their* words.

Designer questions are customized for the situation you are in. An example would be someone not showing an interest in your product or service. Why not ask them, "At this time in your life, right now, what are you looking for"? Answering this question will get them off their negative thinking and on to what's most important to them. Endorphins will flow and rapport will be established, opening the door for you to share your ideas with them. This can be accomplished only by external listening.

Each evening, review how many times you did or didn't focus on the other person during each of the conversations you had that day. You'll know how much internal dialogue is going on inside of you and how much work you still need to do on yourself. Remember, you can give only what you have, so always start with you—*know yourself!* This, in itself, is a lifelong process. Continually ask yourself questions. Respond to them and practice external listening with yourself first, so you can be generous in giving yourself away to others.

The *fourth step* in developing the art of asking questions is to *discover the best outcome for the person with whom you're communicating.* There will always be an outcome for everything you think, say, do, and feel. Befriend the other person and do your best to understand his or her needs and wants. Listen intently, use the other person's words to tune in your responses, and you'll create rapport. This makes it safe for that person to be with you. It opens the door for him or her to discover an appropriate solution through answering the questions you ask. An example of this would be, "I just don't see the value of what you're offering." Take the key word from what they said and ask a follow-up question like, "What value are you looking for?" Another example is, the person says, "None of that is important to me." You could ask, "What *is* most important to you?"

As you continue asking questions, the outcome to your conversation may change based on how the person responds. Keep the exchange going by asking questions so you can uncover any consciously or unconsciously hidden agendas that may provide you with the core criteria needed for the best outcome for that person. This could mean mentally filing information that may not be appropriate to address at this particular time.

If you're dead set on obtaining *your own* personal outcome, you won't hear what the other person is saying. You'll miscommunicate and disconnect. You'll lose the opportunity to have an EEI—*elegant, exquisite,* and *irresistible*—outcome.

This brings us to the *fifth and final step* in developing the art of asking questions: *sensing.* When you take your eyes off yourself and totally focus on others, you'll know when you see, hear, or feel something special that, initially, may not make sense. Have you ever just known something was going to happen, what way to turn, or knew just what to say at just the right time? This is called sensing. There's no logical reasoning involved; you just know that you know. Sensing is noticing that something is going on. You can do this through sight, sound, and touch.

Sensing is knowing when to pause, ask a question, share something about yourself, allow silence, bring up filed information, go more in-depth, use a particular tone of voice, shift your body or be still, pace, lead, be more spontaneous, and increase rapport. It's like Hugh Prather said, "As long as I am trying to decide, I cannot *feel* what I want to do."

Pacing is going along with the person at their level. If they speak slowly, you need to speak slowly. Leading is directing the conversation or suggesting a next step. Use this when someone tells you no: "I can understand that might not be of interest to you. However have you ever thought about...?"

Create questions that are EEI— elegant, exquisite, and irresistible.

The above five steps are the foundational elements to the art of asking questions. As you learn and practice them, both intellectually and emotionally, you'll be on your way to becoming more effective in your business and personal relationships. Be sure to be involved in a lifelong learning program that includes all of your senses! What are you reading every day? How many growth-inducing audios are you listening to daily? Do you attend at least two learning functions every year? How do you experience fun? Are you playful? Do you allow your childlikeness to emerge? What makes you most alive? What is your dream? Have you learned to let certain things you cannot change to just be, and accept them as they are? Who are your mentors? What skills do you have, what skills do you want to master, and how do you or will you use them to benefit others?

As you are developing your abilities in and practicing the art of asking questions, constantly refine these five primary skills:

1. Ask questions with self-esteem. Boost your own and others self-esteem, which is necessary for asking effective questions.

2. Be aware of the impact words have on yourself and others; choose the appropriate words at the appropriate time. (This is called wordsmithing.)

3. Listen externally. (Quiet your internal dialogue and totally listen to what the other person is saying.)

4. Discover the best outcomes for the person with whom you're communicating.

5. Develop your sensing skills by taking your eyes off yourself, while totally focusing on the other person or people.

—Chapter Two—

What's in It for You?

S o what's in it for you? How would you like to benefit? Do you have some specific reasons for reading this book? Take a moment now to write down what you perceive might be the benefits of asking questions. The more specific you are, the deeper your learning experience will be.

Remember, the quality of your life is determined by the questions you ask. The possibilities for your life are opened or closed by the questions you ask. The money you earn is related to the quality of the questions you ask.

Ask yourself these three questions:

1. What three things do I want to accomplish now to improve my ability in asking questions?

2. What three things would I like to accomplish over the next twelve months as a result of more effectively asking questions?

3. How would I like to be using these skills five, ten, fifteen years from now?

If you're reading this book as a generalist, that's okay. You may say, "I'm just open to the possibilities, and I'll accept whatever comes out of it." That's great! So why not challenge yourself? After all, you have to live with yourself, be it at home, at your job or business, with friends, and everywhere you go. You need to apply these ideas on your own or they won't do you any good. Reading this book is easy and may make you feel good. So what will you do when you put it down? What will you do the next time you talk with someone? How will you communicate from here on out?

What Outcomes Do You Want?

To assist you in discovering more about the outcomes you want, take a few moments now to answer the following questions. Focus your attention on the broadest perspective you can for each question, then relax and let your subconscious answer them.

1. What's your purpose in reading this book?

2. How much time have you invested in previous learning experiences to better internalize and utilize the ideas presented?

3. How many mentors have you had in your life, and what did they do for you?

4. Do you have five skills that can help you earn more money? Write them down.

5. What's been your greatest learning experience during the last five, ten years?

6. Have you invested in your lifelong learning during the last five years? List specific details: books, audios, videos, DVDs, courses, coaching, mentors, conventions, seminars, programs, training, or academics.

7. What's your ultimate ideal career or business and life situation?

8. Do you have a plan to double, triple, quadruple, or quintuple your income over the next three to five years?

9. What's your greatest skill and how much money has it earned for you during the last twelve months?

10. What value, from zero to a hundred percent, do you place on emotional income versus monetary income?

11. Are you prepared for the "what ifs" in your life? For example, what if you get fired, quit, your company is merged, or there's a downsizing?

12. Do you have a pension or profit-sharing plan?

13. Do you have a personal retirement account?

14. Which of these resources do you have on your success team: doctor, lawyer, stockbroker, financial consultant, nutrition coach, career/business mentor, spiritual adviser, fitness coach, travel consultant, lifelong-learning coach?

15. How would you feel about this philosophy: work a hundred days for money, learn a hundred days, travel a hundred days for fun, and do whatever you want for the other sixty-five?

16. Do you have a book library at home?

17. Do you have a video/DVD/MP3 library?

18. Do you have a music library?

19. Do you have an audio library?

20. Do you have a planner or PDA that you use daily?

21. Do you do a daily self-evaluation on what you did, who you met, what you learned?

22. Do you have a team of like-minded, success-oriented people with whom you associate? How often do you meet and what are the benefits of doing so?

23. Do you fear success?

24. Do you fear failure?

25. What have you done in the last five years to prevent yourself from taking a quantum leap in your relationships, career or business, and income?

26. On a scale of zero to a hundred percent, how would you rate your self-esteem?

27. What does your self-esteem have to do with integrating these questions into your life?

28. After leaving a learning experience, do you act on the biggest and most challenging idea?

29. When you leave a learning experience, do you immediately take sequential, organized, structured steps to gradually build new skills?

30. Who are the one to ten people who have had an influence on your career or business?

31. What legacy do you want to leave behind for having lived your life?

32. What's the poorest outcome you've had in your life?

33. What career choice have you made that sidetracked you from your specifically desired future success?

34. What excuses have you given yourself for not reaching your career or business destination?

35. On a scale of zero to a hundred percent, how comfortable or uncomfortable are you in reading and responding to these questions?

36. How would you complete these statements?
    a. I blame myself most when....
    b. I criticize myself when....
    c. I criticize others when....
    d. I compare myself to....
    e. What I fear most is....

37. Are you in the habit of making agreements and keeping them?

38. Who are the five most influential role models in your life?

39. What would need to exist for you to use these questions to upgrade your relationships and career or business?

You may have just responded briefly to these questions. However, at some time in the near future, answer them in depth. You'll gain more insight into yourself which will serve you in moving forward.

Questions Are Powerful

Questions are powerful and have fifteen basic functions. When asking questions, you involve one or more of them. Questions can:

1. Garner attention.

2. Start a conversation.

3. Help obtain information.

4. Give information.

5. Energize a conversation.

6. Start people thinking.

7. Help bring things to a conclusion.

8. Resolve conflict.

9. Stir a new or neglected desire or dream.

10. Create breakthroughs.

11. Affirm people, thereby showing a genuine interest in them.

12. Create possibilities that didn't exist before.

13. Help people focus on what's important to them.

14. Assist people in overcoming obstacles.

15. Help people see you or what you're doing as the solution to their problem or potential fruition of their objective.

How Can Asking Questions Benefit You?

The more you know the easier it is for you to create your life the way you want it. There are many benefits to be gained by asking questions; thirty-eight possible benefits are:

1. Finding your missing piece.

2. Learning more.

3. Making friends.

4. Eliminating loneliness.

5. Getting a date.

6. Scheduling an appointment.

7. Deepening your relationships.

8. Having superlative communications.

9. Helping people discover and adopt new behavior.

10. Creating curiosity.

11. Being an energy builder.

12. Eliminating criticism.

13. Showing respect for others and yourself.

14. Releasing dogmatic self-centeredness.

15. Increasing productivity.

16. Building harmony.

17. Developing trust.

18. Persuading people.

19. Solving problems.

20. Reducing mistakes.

21. Getting ideas across.

22. Overcoming objections.

23. Obtaining cooperation.

24. Clarifying instructions.

25. Reducing anxiety.

26. Gaining rapport.

27. Exploring the world of ideas.

28. Receiving a promotion.

29. Going to the next level in your business.

30. Making a deep impact.

31. Developing external listening skills.

32. Obtaining faster outcomes.

33. Enhancing self-esteem.

34. Eliminating ambiguity.

35. Increasing morale.

36. Generating discovery learning.

37. Selling more.

38. Enjoying conversations.

Be sure to add to this list as you discover more of *your* specific benefits in asking questions.

Eight Suggestions to Help You Get the Outcomes You Want

These suggestions require their own skill development and need to blend with self-esteem:

1. *Know what you really need, want, and value.* Do you know what you need, want, and value? In order to get what you really, really want, you first need to know the specific outcomes you desire. What's your intention? Will you know it when you see, hear, or feel it? In order to know you have what you need, want, and value, you need to be able to *identify* it and *recognize* it as such!

A need is something that's vital for survival; you can't live without it. Examples would be food, water, and oxygen. A want, however, enhances life and is culturally influenced. You may need transportation and understand that walking can get you to your destination. However, you may want a new Mercedes. We value what's desirable for its own sake; it's important to us. And what we value differs for each of us; what's important to one is not necessarily important to another. Some value relationships above all else. Others, to their detriment, don't care about their relationships and value them only when they stand to lose them. Of three people who value education, one may interpret this as acquiring a Ph.D., another may simply want a high school diploma, and yet a third may choose to learn just by overcoming challenging experiences.

First meet your basic needs, then you'll be enabled to go beyond that toward someone or something you want or value. For example, say you're flying in an airliner with a small child when cabin pressure is suddenly lost and the oxygen masks drop down. What's the best thing to do? Put the oxygen mask on yourself first (a need for survival) before putting one on the child (someone you value). You wouldn't be able to help the child if you were to go unconscious!

2. *Asking questions is 90 percent planning and preparation, 10 percent execution.* It's what you do for yourself inside before you ask questions that helps determine the outcomes you'll have with others. You're always getting outcomes, so wouldn't it be great to design questions appropriate to obtaining the outcomes you need, want, and value, while assisting others in doing the same?

It's what you do for yourself inside before you ask questions that helps determine the outcomes you'll have with others.

Someone once asked me a question which I chose not to respond to—simply because of the way he asked it. Have you ever done that? I chose not to respond because the question was not appropriately designed to where I would have felt comfortable communicating with that person.

3. *Know the beginnings, transitions, and intended endings.*
Before you begin asking questions of someone, know what you
intend to accomplish. Obviously, you can't know the exact outcome, and *you certainly don't want to be attached to any
particular results*. So in any conversation, always strive for an
outcome that works best for the person you're talking with, as
well as for you. Go for a win/win, based on the information he or
she shares with you.

Here are five key questions that can bring about a conclusion
in all kinds of situations:

1. What needs to exist for you to...?

2. Now that you know the possible solutions, how would you like
   to proceed with…?

3. Would you like to go ahead with…?

4. Is it possible that…?

5. May I suggest this…?

There are often transitions during a conversation. Can you
recognize them? Are you prepared to keep asking questions that
will help the other person focus on their most desired outcomes?
You have only one chance to get a relationship off to a good start.
So how is that best done? Do you begin conversations in a
friendly way? For example, you could say, "Hello, Jack (use the
person's name whenever possible), it's really great to see you!"

Do your opening communications show you care about and
are taking an interest in the other person? Recall something about
the last time you spoke to a particular individual. Then find out
about something important that's currently going on in their life.
This affirms them—says they are valuable. For example you
might say, "Last time we spoke your father was going to have
surgery. How did that go?" What impact do you want to have on

him or her by your beginning conversation? How will you focus on the other person and engage them in conversation?

4. *Conversations without gaps.* Have you ever been in a conversation and found you weren't connecting with the other person? To avoid gaps in a conversation, remember to start where people are, not where you want them to be. Talk to them at their level of reception. Ask questions around *their* ideas, interests, needs, wants, values, and topics. Take a key word or phrase of *theirs* and design a question around it. Let's say the key is, "I'm not ready now." You could ask "What are you ready for?" If you ignore their concern or objection and move outside of it, you'll create a break or gap in communication.

Ask questions by using *their* words and *their* way of expressing them. Make the questions so appropriate to the other person that he or she won't even realize you stimulated them into opening up to you. Since you listen a lot, that person will like you and love answering your questions. Don't be surprised if they even start giving you their life story! Once some people get started they keep going. Let them talk themselves out—clear their slate—then they're likely to be more receptive to what you have to say.

5. *Ask someone who knows.* When you don't know something, what do you do? What if there's someone you can go to for the answer? Do you seek their guidance? Do you regularly read educational or motivational materials, listen to uplifting mind- or spirit-enriching audios, and attend learning programs? Are you filling your mind with great ideas and acting on them? Or do you keep doing the same things while, somehow, expecting new and different outcomes? That's impossible! Find someone who knows and ask for your missing piece of information.

As you converse with others, be aware that they have certain abilities. Have you discovered what they are? Are you interested in learning more about their skills? Asking questions can help you and others discover and find missing pieces. Have you noticed that when people discover and learn new things for themselves, the impact is greater and the information is more likely to be incorporated into their lives? Would you like to have this happen more often in your life? Wouldn't it be great if you could help it happen for others as well?

6. *Give value*. Recall that we value what's important to us. How do you discover the value of others? What can you do, be, and say that will cause them to feel valued? Do you value yourself? How do you show others you value them?

Have you ever been given undivided attention because you first valued the other person by asking questions and then listening to them? Were you ever so engrossed in the conversation that three or four hours seemed like twenty minutes? Did you find that conversation of value? Why? What was it about that conversation that was so rewarding?

One of the ingredients of valuing others is the words we use. Our words communicate what we value. Become a wordsmith—a *master* wordsmith! A master wordsmith gives undivided attention by using the words (and lingo) of the other person and moving steadily forward in the conversation, creating elegant, exquisite, and irresistible outcomes. The master's tools include self-esteem, external listening, and asking questions.

The next time you're in a major discussion or negotiation ask yourself the following questions: How's my self-esteem and how is theirs? What are they really saying to me now? What question(s) could I ask to bring us onto the same page—to grow to a mutual understanding?

When a master wordsmith is in conversation with someone, that someone senses the wordsmith's genuine interest and feels valued. He or she feels validated and honored because the wordsmith is focusing on the other person's needs, wants, and values. The master wordsmith assists the other person by asking questions to discover the outcomes that are best for him or her. When the conversation is completed, the other person feels and knows that he or she is lovable, capable, whole, and in charge of his or her own life, with needs, wants, values, and self-esteem in place.

7. *Ask with congruency and believe in what you're doing.* You're being congruent when the things you think, say, do, and feel are done with such wholehearted conviction they are communicating the exact same thing. Sensing your clarity, others will then be more inclined to respond honestly to your questions. Have you ever felt uncomfortable while someone was speaking, even though you believed the words they were saying? Did you sense that the speaker was unsure or didn't really believe what they were saying was true?

We communicate 7 percent with the words we use, 38 percent with our voice, and 55 percent with body language—93 percent of our communication is nonverbal! If our words, voice, and behavior are incongruent, we give the listener a mixed message, and he or she won't believe us. We retain and learn most what we talk about and share with others. Asking people questions gets them to talk—and then they learn!

Before you ask someone else a question, ask yourself the same question and be clear about the answer. Since you can only give what you have, you can only ask others with congruency based on how you have already asked and responded to yourself.

For example, how can you best answer other people's objections? By first answering your own! "Know thyself!" If you don't believe in whatever you're offering someone else, be it an idea, product, service, or opportunity, how could you possibly expect anyone else to believe in it?

8. Just *ask, ask, ask.* Ask until you receive the outcome you want which, in a general sense, is to get to the bottom of it. (Of course, you may want the other person to say "Yes!" to whatever you are suggesting, even though that may not always be the outcome.) Some people call this peeling the onion. Keep asking questions until you get to the core of the other person's objection. If you don't get to the essence of their concern, it probably means you don't yet have the skill or the desire to keep going. You're not asking questions to be obnoxious and bowl people over. You simply want to sincerely connect with everyone you meet so you can reach them while creating a win/win situation.

Most of us were public speakers until we were three, and then we were told, "Shut up!" How are three-year-olds? They're typically open, innocent, blunt, curious, interested, and never give up. What do they do? They ask questions, their favorite being "Why?"; "Why, Daddy?"; or "Why, Mommy?" Why this and why that? Three-year-olds want to know more about *everything*. However, they don't have the understanding and vocabulary skill to couch their words so they can obtain the outcomes they want. Gradually their spirit and self-esteem are destroyed by comments like, "Shut up. It's none of your business."; "Will you ever be quiet?"; "Stop asking so many questions." Their questions are ignored—as being unimportant. Before too long, the children begin feeling unimportant and stop asking questions. By age five their spontaneity, inquisitiveness, and creativity are virtually destroyed. Later, when they're teenagers, they may have learned to deflect others by saying, "I don't know."; "Everything's fine."; or "You just don't understand." This can lead to very sad endings, as we've all seen on the news.

If those we regarded as significant paid no attention or shut us down when we were little, we learned to go elsewhere to have our needs met. For example, teenagers usually turn to their peers. Has this ever happened to you? How would you like to recapture the curiosity you had as a three-year-old, coupled with the skill of asking questions? Then ask, ask, ask until you're satisfied, and be willing to make mistakes while never giving up! Most people stop before they obtain the outcomes they want because they aren't willing to make mistakes or deal with rejection. They fear looking silly or appearing stupid. They don't give themselves enough time to refine their skills and discover the appropriate questions. This is a self-esteem issue.

Ask questions to sincerely connect with everyone you meet, so you can reach them while creating a win/win situation.

When was the last time you asked for a raise or promotion? Have you ever had a relationship struggle where you needed to let someone know about their insensitive behavior? Have you ever needed to tell someone something they really didn't want to hear? Has anyone ever loved you enough to ask you questions that helped you discover, for yourself, some blind spots or areas where you have been inadvertently making mistakes?

Have you ever started asking questions to learn someone's position on something and gotten to the point where you knew they weren't going to like what was taking place? Did you then pull back and change the direction of the conversation? Is it possible, at that precise moment, that they lost the opportunity to grow and discover more about themselves? We've all had these experiences to one degree or another. It's best to complete the direction in which the conversation is going rather than avoiding the issue, which could lead to a misunderstanding later.

This is where self-esteem and asking questions comes into play. Until you have self-esteem, you won't be comfortable putting yourself in uncomfortable situations. You won't believe you can handle it. Fortunately, the more you practice the more likely you'll be able to ask the appropriate questions at the appropriate time.

When you learn and integrate these skills in questioning yourself first, you'll discover the greatness you were born with and what makes you most alive. As you continually practice the eight suggestions covered in this chapter, both with yourself and others, you'll develop the skills to master the art of asking questions. You'll be empowered to better connect with the people you meet and move forward more quickly in life.

—Chapter Three—

Creating Communication Acceptance

Remember, as we talked about before, when you start conversing with someone, begin where they are, not where you want them to be. People like responding to questions—as long as they concern them, their work, their family, or their interests. Starting where they are gives you the best opportunity to get their attention. Listen closely to the person and observe their behavior. If you're in front of them you can pick up cues of how ready they are to talk. Do they seem relaxed, receptive, or frustrated and talking in a hurried manner? Listen for what is not being said between the lines of their words. Then match your tone of voice and energy level with theirs. When you create an atmosphere of harmony, the other person tends to feel safe, secure, and comfortable. This leads to establishing rapport, which can be present in any of the following six levels of communication:

1. *Trivia*—This level of communication deals with unimportant matters. So even though it's just casual, passive conversation can still be used to build rapport. When you converse in this manner you use clichés such as, "How are things going?" or "What do you think about this weather?" Sharing trivia, or small talk, with someone new can be incredibly effective in starting a relationship. It helps establish rapport.

2. People Talk—This is the usual lunchtime or having-a-cup-of-coffee-together type of conversation. Events, people, and happenings are discussed only superficially; you tell only what others have been doing rather than sharing who you are and how you feel. Frequently, the facts of the conversation are distorted by a lack of complete or correct information. An example would be, "Let me tell you about Tom and Mary," or "Did you hear about the car the Joneses bought?" Tabloid papers, soap operas, and serial movies on television—including media-hyped interests of high profile people—are all famous for their people talk. There's a large segment of society that's hooked on and stuck at the people-talk level of communication. Gossip would fall into this category.

3. Opinions—Here's where people give their points of view and beliefs about things. At this level, you're willing to expose some of the inner you, with the possibility of being criticized or having a disagreement. However, at the first sign of rejection, if your self-esteem is lacking, you may go back to the first two levels or say what you think the other person wants you to say. Some examples are: "What's your opinion about...?"; "I believe that needs to be handled in ...."; "I think the President, King, Queen, Prime Minister (or another prominent individual) needs to...."

4. Ideas—Here's where you discuss concepts and thoughts. The left brain's logic is deeply involved. Ideas are plentiful; of course, however, it's only the ideas you act on that can make a difference in your life. People who like to share ideas often form a networking group of creative, outcome-directed, productive, competent, achieving individuals. Others may create a discussion group that meets once a month, where they go more in-depth and share their thoughts on a particular idea. Conversations around ideas may begin with: "What one idea made the most sense to you today?"; "How will you use it to maximize your potential?"; or "One idea I had was...." These are usually results-oriented types of communications, although it's possible each person could come up with his or her own conclusion.

5. *Feelings*—This is the condition of being emotionally affected. Feelings is a generic term comprised of sensation, desire, and emotion, excluding perception and thought. No two people can have the exact same feelings because everyone is unique, as is their own personal history. You may have the same background and similar experiences, however, it's impossible to have the exact same feelings as someone else.

There's also a difference between your emotions talking and talking about your feelings. When your emotions talk you are *expressing*. An example is if you scream, yell, and put your kids down by saying such things as: "You'll never amount to anything!"; "You're so stupid!"; "When will you ever learn?"; "Sit down and shut up, you're making so much noise, I can't even think!" These indicate that something is going on inside of you; however, often no one knows what that something is—including you! Your kids, in such instances, regardless of their behavior, are the recipients of your frustration. It's not about them, even though it may appear to be. Unfortunately, kids often carry these messages for life. This behavior destroys communication and devastates their self-esteem.

On the other hand, when talking about your feelings, you *describe* what is going on with you. Instead of screaming and yelling, you say, "I'm tired. I've had a rough day at work. Three people were out sick. I just need to have a few minutes of peace and quiet. Would you mind playing in the other room until dinner? Thanks, I appreciate your understanding and cooperation."

At the feelings level of conversation, you talk honestly and courageously about how you feel by sharing your doubts, fears, frustrations, angers, joys, and heartaches—about yourself and who you feel you are inside. This behavior serves you and, by example, teaches others how to describe *their* feelings. You begin to know yourself and others better. You grow and help others know themselves better, too, because you let them know you. When you have self-esteem, it's easier to begin all communications at this level.

You are comfortable beginning all conversations with: "How do you feel about...?"

6. *Plateau*—This is where you're perfectly in tune and in harmony with another person. You communicate with empathy, understanding, and depth, and each of you enjoys mutually beneficial emotional satisfaction. You're alive and full of energy, and time seems to fly by. A typical question and subsequent comments would be: "Do you realize we've been talking for two hours, yet it feels like only two minutes? I feel like I've known you all my life. I really look forward to getting together with you again!"

As you review these six levels of communication, recall your own behavior. Where do you spend most of your time? Are you receiving the outcomes you want when you communicate? Have you been open and honest about the feelings going on inside you? Are you aware of what those feelings are?

Assuming you could create your communications the way you want them, how would you like your conversations to *be*? Have you ever had plateau communications with others? Would you be interested in creating more of them? Where do you feel the majority of people in our culture are with their level of communication? More importantly, where are *you* with *your* level of communication?

All levels of communication are necessary. It would be impossible to communicate at the plateau level twenty-four hours a day. We all need relaxation and regrouping time. The first four levels: trivia, people talk, opinions, and ideas, prepare you and the other person for the last two levels. Yet, the last two—*feelings* and *plateau*—create all of your meaningful communications and in-depth relationships.

Recall your most gratifying relationships and you may discover that you've already established some mutually beneficial empathic relationships. Would you like more? The rewards are great but, remember, it's all a process and it takes time. Be patient with yourself and others.

Defining and Reflecting for Better Understanding

Before we move onto gaining more core knowledge, let's clarify some definitions. To better understand the message I'm sharing, let's do our own wordsmithing together, making sure we are in agreement term-wise. The following words, some of which we've used before, are key to many of the concepts being shared in this book. Feel comfortable in making them your own and consider your answers to the question(s) posed at the end of each definition.

- *Climate*—the nature of your attitude and demeanor, which determines the atmosphere you create in and around you. This is a result of how you feel about yourself. Is this the climate you set? With self-esteem you create a climate of acceptance and inclusion.

- *Congruent*—when what you think, feel, say, and do are in harmony; absent of contradiction. How congruent are you every day?

- *Energy*—internal and inherent power, potential force; capacity for vigorous action; with force, capability; with vigor, health; the idea of activity. So how healthy, capable, and active are you? What is your energy level on a daily basis? Do you need to increase it?

- *External Listening*—hearing what a person is saying by being totally present and focused on him or her, with nothing going on inside you; your mind is quiet. You're not conducting any internal dialogue. You're not thinking about what to say next. You're honestly listening to the other person. Remember, you can't learn anything when you're talking—only when you're listening! How well are you listening?

- *Five-Sensing*—experiencing the here and now through sight, sound, taste, touch, and smell. It's a full experience, on a moment-by-moment basis. Our two most developed senses are sight and hearing, but feelings arise from all five. They're influential in helping us make decisions. How is your five-sensing? Are you getting just bits and pieces of it because you're always racing to the future rather than enjoying the present moment?

- *Leading*—conducting, guiding, preceding, directing, influencing. Leading is empowering others into developing new behaviors and activities. People will follow your lead only to the extent to which you have rapport with them. How are your leading skills?

- *Outcome*—that which comes out of or results from doing something: the conclusion, the result, the consequence. We always receive an outcome for everything we think, say, do, and feel. Are you getting the outcome you want?

- *Pacing*—rate of movement. Matching your verbal rate, words, subject matter, tone of voice, and body language to the person with whom you are speaking. It helps people relate, identify, and perceive. Pacing is used to help establish rapport. Do you invest the time to establish rapport?

- *Question*—an inquiry or interrogation that shows you're interested in learning more about the other person or subject matter. Are you more likely to ask a question or revert the conversation to a topic about yourself?

- *Alternative Questions*—an inquiry or interrogation that gives people definitive choices, for example, "Would you prefer audience participation or a straight lecture?" These are closed questions. The listener needs to choose one alternative or the other—there's no indication of other possibilities or invitation for further discussion. How open and flexible are you in your inquiries?

- *Clarifying Questions*—inquiries that ask for supportive data based on a general statement that is made. Asking for explanations, evidence, or examples, for instance, "What do you base that on?" or "What did you mean when you said...?" "Please expand on what you were saying when...?" Or "I understand your point. What would need to exist for us to...?" These are used in open-ended, interview-type, and congruent questions. How courageous are you in asking clarifying questions and working toward the outcomes you really want?

- **Hypothetical Questions**—invite the person to evaluate his/her own position or perspective and share it. They can help a person think and see his or her situation more clearly which can light the way to providing something to them, sharing an idea, or working together in some way. Begin with "Just suppose..., then what...?" or "What if...?" These are used in open-ended and interview questions. Do you use hypothetical questions to discover how you can best serve others?

- **Mirroring Questions**—this is more of a restatement of what the other person has said than a question in its own right. Done well, they invite the other person to go on, to say more. They're used mostly in open-ended questions. An example is when someone may say, "I just got the job done!" You could mirror back to them the question, "You just got the job done?" "Yes," they reply. "I stayed up all night and just got it done." Then the person can share what their perception is of what they've told you, which may or may not reflect your understanding of the matter. Mirror to gain mutual clarity.

- **Probing Questions**—dig deeper into a person's statement to acquire added insight and understanding. They're used at the open-ended, interview, and congruent level of asking questions. An example is, "Can you tell me more about what you're looking for?" Do you probe sufficiently to get beyond the superficial?

- **Qualifying Questions**—used to bring a statement into perspective in relation to its results. For example, "How will this benefit you?"; "What will we get out of this?"; "What will the long-term result of this be?" These are used in open-ended, interview, and congruent questions. Do you ask yourself and others qualifying questions?

- ***Rapport***—a relationship of harmony, agreement, accord, affinity. To the degree that you and I are in agreement with each other, verbally and nonverbally, we are in a state of rapport. Do you regularly experience rapport with others?

These definitions provide some of the foundational knowledge needed to obtain EEI (elegant, exquisite, and irresistible) outcomes—the purpose of asking questions. When you're listening to someone and you're not clear about what he or she is saying, ask for clarification. Otherwise, what was said and your interpretation of it may be totally different. Your asking shows that you're listening externally and want to understand. That person will learn you are interested in them and what they're saying. You may observe a relaxing in their facial features and a brightening in their eyes.

Five Affirmations that Can Help You Ask Better Questions

There are five affirmations that can serve to help you incorporate asking questions into your life. These were revised from the work of Grace Pilon from the Workshop Way. Say them at least three times a day: once in the morning, once during the day, and right before going to sleep. When you hear them, you will, at some level, know they are true.

1. I'm smart.

2. I'm intelligent.

3. It's acceptable for me to make mistakes. I use them as opportunities to learn.

4. It's acceptable for me to ask for help. I ask for my missing piece.

5. It's acceptable for me to not learn everything now. (The conscious mind can hold only from three to nine pieces of information at one time.)

Again, repeat these affirmations three times a day for the next thirty days, and watch what happens. Post them on your bathroom mirror, refrigerator, in the car, and at work. Gradually, you'll develop feelings around them. As you practice them, you will also develop new behaviors. This is what is meant by "knowledge plus sensory experience equals new behavior." However, just because you know something intellectually doesn't mean a whole lot. As someone wise said, "To know and not to do is worse than not knowing." For example, there are many people with Ph.D.s who are not applying their knowledge. Then there are others, like Walt Disney, who, with very little formal education, created worlds that are visited daily.

Involve Your *Feelings*

In order to integrate any body of knowledge into your behavior, including how to ask questions, you need to involve your feelings. Then, and only then, will that knowledge become a part of you. You'll have a fire in your belly, and the excitement and energy to *do* something with the knowledge you *have*!

When you ask questions, both of yourself and others, feelings emerge and they need to be described in order for appropriate action to take place. If feelings go undescribed when they need to be described, they'll be expressed at some other time, in some other way. And it's possible that this some other time and way may not be the most appropriate. Have you ever been in a conversation knowing something else needed to be said in order for the other person to effectively move forward to take appropriate action, but you didn't have the knowledge, skill, or self-esteem to say it? Unfortunately, this is an all too common occurrence.

Many have learned to minimize and bury their feelings. Since they were children, they've been told, "Grow up! Stop crying. You're a big boy/girl now." As adults, we've often heard statements like: "It's no big deal.", "You'll get over it.", "I don't care how you feel; just get the job done.", "Don't bring your problems to work.", "There's no reason to be afraid." As a result, we've learned that to share feelings is unacceptable and we began stuffing them and numbing out. We wondered why no one understood us, and we rationalized about how things didn't work out the way we had planned.

We can only disguise, deny, or rationalize our feelings for a limited period of time. Feelings stay with us until we deal with them. The body stores all of our feelings. If we choose not to describe them and let our feelings run their natural course, our bodies will let us know through sleeplessness, high blood pressure, nervousness, and other disorders, all of which can lead to disease! Some people also choose to numb out through addictions—drugs, sex, alcohol, food, shopping, television, loud music, travel, the Internet, and such.

Have the Courage to Describe Your *Feelings*

Feelings have a language all their own. Do you find it difficult, at times, to describe yours? Are you uncomfortable around people when they're describing theirs? Have you ever felt uncomfortable, yet didn't quite know how to put your feelings into words? I certainly have! I also recognize that I'll never have it all together with my feelings. They're constantly evolving as I grow, mature, develop new skills, and live life. There are times when I have ambivalent feelings. I'll never know or have processed all of my feelings, nor will anyone else. We're all constantly in process. We know we are alive when we're feeling. Our feelings take into account what we've been experiencing and let us know if it was painful, pleasurable, or a mixture of both. We all need to consider refining and broadening our feeling vocabulary. Author Reuel L. Howe says, "Dialogue is to love what blood is to the body. When the flow of blood stops the body dies. When dialogue stops love dies and resentment and hatred are born. Communication can mean life or death."

Now stop reading for a moment, be quiet, and notice the feeling words that come to mind. Write them down! Feel free to include such words as: This is stupid. How ridiculous. What will this do? What is he up to? This is silly. Just give me the five easy steps to the art of asking questions. Give yourself permission to write whatever comes up.

After you've made yourself more aware of your words, ask yourself: "How else can I describe what I've noticed? What other words can mean the same or similar things? How different is the feeling I have as a result?" If you've made statements, examine the words in your comments and ask yourself a question like: "What does silly feel like?" Use your thesaurus and begin creating a list of feeling words. When you're at a seminar or if you get a chance to view a documentary, listen for the feeling words used by the speaker or narrator. What feelings came up for you in response to those words? This observation can help you improve your communication skills, increasing your ability to connect with others. After you've done these feelings exercises, go to the back of the book for more feeling words to incorporate into your questions.

Listen for and Respond to Other People's *Feelings* by Asking Caring Questions

To communicate most effectively with others, listen for and respond to their feelings—not the event or circumstances. Most of the time, unfortunately, people respond with statements that de-energize the person, causing them to go round and round. For example, a child comes home from school, moping around saying, "Everyone else is in a group except me. No matter what I do, nobody likes me. I try, but they just don't like me." An adult's immediate response might be: "There are lots of children at school and in the neighborhood; forget about the others." Or, "That happened to me when I was your age. Things will change. You'll get over it. Just give it some time." Or, "You're a great kid. Just be yourself and take the first step. Invite them to do something with you. Don't let them get to you." While all of these responses are well-intended, they deal only with the event or circumstances, rather than the feelings. Notice that they're all statements rather then questions.

Listen for and respond to other people's feelings.

Now, instead of responding with de-energizing statements, let's respond to the feelings with caring questions. For example, you could ask, "Does not being part of a group feel lonely or like you're an outcast? Do you feel hurt when you're excluded, rejected, or left alone—no matter what you say or do?" The goal here is to create an atmosphere where the child can describe what it feels like to be left out or disliked. Children and adults are more willing to open up and respond when they're asked thoughtful questions. They feel as though somebody cares enough to hear their concerns, and that they're finally being understood.

Go on and use your knowledge, understanding, and skill in asking questions to help a child or an adult discover a solution for him- or herself. When you respond to feelings instead of circumstances and events, respect is given, trust is established, mutual understanding takes place, the relationship moves forward, and the child or adult feels better about him- or herself.

David Viscott, a well-known psychiatrist and author, says, "Feelings are our reaction to what we perceive through our senses and, in turn, they color and define our perception of the world. Feelings, in fact, *are* the world we live in. They shape our reaction to what we will experience in the future. Understanding feelings is the key to the mastery of ourselves and finding true independence, as well as giving us the ability to better relate with others.

"When we lose touch with our feelings, we lose touch with our most human qualities. When we live in our feelings, we are most in touch, most alive. The more honest you are, the more energy you'll have to deal with the challenges that arise. Being in touch with your feelings is the only way you can ever become your best self, the only way you can become open and free, the only way you can become your own person." All of this is available to you and others simply by asking questions.

The Five Types of Questions

There are five types of questions involved in the art of asking questions:

1. Safe.
2. Closed.
3. Open.
4. Interview.
5. Congruent.

We'll discuss each type of question, and give examples and much more in the following chapters. Each type of question is unique and meets the various needs, wants, and values of people and represents a different level of communication. Each allows us to retain our personal power with utmost integrity and gain more clarity as we discover for ourselves the outcomes we really want. We can then assist others in doing the same.

—Chapter Four—

Safe Questions

The first level of questions are safe ones, simplistic and virtually effortless. They contain nothing that could elicit fear. Safe questions comfortably draw out information from others. They're relaxing and easy to answer. People feel comfortable with you, tension is released, and conversational flow begins. The responses don't require deep thought, technical analysis, or mathematical computation. Safe questions create comfort and ease.

Have you ever been at a family, business, or social gathering when you were unsure of how to begin a conversation? Did you feel uncomfortable, awkward, out of place? With practice, you can begin all of your communications by using safe questions. Two "McGranisms" that can help you in creating a climate of acceptance are:

1. Go in and out of people's worlds on their terms, not yours. Have you heard of the cliché, "When in Rome do as the Romans do"? Be in relationship with people and stay in conversation with them at the level, topic, and amount they would like to have with you. Do things and have conversations *their* way.

2. Start where people are, not where you want them to be. Talk with people at *their* emotional level and on *their* level of receptivity.

First, "five-sense" the environment. Be aware of what you see, hear, smell, touch, and taste within the entire area. Can you initiate a conversation or continue it by asking a question about any unique item in the surroundings, perhaps something that might be of special interest to the other person? Sense the atmosphere and note the energy level of the individual with whom you are talking. Stay within that person's comfort zone with your voice tone, words, body language, and pace of speaking—and stand no closer than an arm's length. Listen to what is being said, as well as to what's not being said, by observing the other person's attitude and body language; then ask your first safe question. The other person is likely to feel at ease and readily respond.

You may think you don't need to behave this way with people you know; however, that couldn't be any further from the truth. Don't take anyone for granted, especially family and friends. Every day we all add to our personal history through our experiences and knowledge gained, plus everything we think, say, do, and feel. Our awareness expands. The more adventurous we are in meeting new people, going to new places, doing new things, the more this is true.

Do you attempt to discover new things about those you know? Or do you just assume there's nothing more to learn about them? If they were to die tomorrow, would there be anything else you'd wish you knew about them? When you honestly care about others and choose to continue to learn more about everyone who comes into your world, doing so in a thoughtful manner, you create a safe place for them to discover more about themselves. Gradually, people will recognize that no matter what's going on in their world, it's safe to be with you because you're truly interested in them as people—not just for a perceived gain you may realize by having them associate with you. Safe questions go something like this:

- Where do you live?
- How long have you lived there?
- Have you seen...?

- How do you know...?
- What's happening?
- What's going on?

To help you discover where you are with safe questions, stop reading and write down five to ten safe questions. This will benchmark your present skill. If you're having a tough time coming up with safe questions, ask yourself, "What am I holding onto that's preventing me from doing so? What do I need to let go of to be able to create some safe questions? What is it about my present self-talk that may be preventing me from moving forward with this?"

If you still aren't able to write some safe questions, write down the answers to the questions just posed. This enables you to free yourself of what's going on inside you now to make room in your mind so you can respond differently. If you're not comfortable doing this with your current skills, rest assured you'll receive some fine payoffs as you refine them. Eventually, you'll be able to create safe questions acceptable in all kinds of situations. When people *easily* respond to your safe questions, you'll know you're being effective with them.

The key benefit of safe questioning is establishing trust. People need to be assured of your integrity before they'll be comfortable responding to you. It's something they'll just sense, which you can assure by giving them TUA—total unconditional acceptance. Creating trust requires making sure that what you think, say, and do are one and the same. Then people will see you as whole, recognizing and knowing that what you appear to be on the outside is in harmony with who you are on the inside.

Safe questions can be taken for granted because they're so easy. How well you create a safe environment for people determines how willing they'll be to engage in conversation with you. To make things even easier, let's make the word SAFE into an acrostic. We'll give each of the four letters of the word safe the first letter of a significant aspect of creating the rapport necessary for people to feel more comfortable with you.

S stands for Secure. Everyone has a desire to feel safe, secure, and familiar. For example, why do children, and even adults, love to hear the same stories over and over again? The repetition and comfort of knowing the endings creates reassurance. When a person feels secure in your presence, he or she is willing to let you into their world. So what constitutes security to another? Self-esteem, comfort zones, and risk factors all determine how secure individuals feel. Just ask someone later on today what speed they consider to be driving fast. For one person it could be 45 or 65 mph, while for someone who's a racecar driver, it could be 220! How about you? What speed do you consider to be fast?

Ask someone who's used to the speed of a new computer what fast is, then ask another with an old one. Perception is the truth for the individual, and it varies considerably. Pace your questions so you don't take for granted the intense need most people have to feel secure. Look for ways to notice the security needs of others. Whether you're at work, at home, or somewhere else, people give you cues and clues. Learn to pick up on the signals, and adjust your talking speed accordingly.

A stands for Affirm. When people are genuinely affirmed, they feel safe being themselves. Match their speed, tone, and energy. Compliment them for who they are, what they're doing, or what you see them endeavoring to accomplish. Ask yourself, "What do I appreciate about this person?" Share what comes to you in a way that will allow that person to feel your sincerity. For example, you could say, "One of the things I enjoy about you is how open you are to hear new ideas. You have demonstrated this by the way you've taken action on what I shared with you."

Recall times when people were trying to sell you something. Were you able to tell the difference between the sales representatives who were genuinely interested in you and your needs and wants versus those who were just going through their superficial sales routine to get your business? When you get into the habit of really affirming people, they feel it and gradually show appreciation by their comfort in answering your questions. You can affirm a person with soft eyes, soft words, soft touch, and a soft heart.

F is for Feelings. Have you discovered how most decisions are made? They are ultimately made on a feeling level, backed up by a little logic or maybe none at all! Successfully creating a safe environment begins when the other person starts feeling you're harmless. Now while you can intellectualize or logic it out all you want, until a person feels safe, they won't come your way.

E stands for Energy. While you're asking a safe question, notice the other person's energy. This will clearly show itself by the number of words they use, the more the better, and how free they feel to say what's on their mind. Their body language will also show you how much energy, or lack of it, they have toward your question. Watch any sporting event when it gets down to the final seconds. Every player is watching every other player's energy to determine what the next play needs to be. Energy begets energy. Pace the energy level of your safe questions with the energy level of the individual.

Remember, if you've asked the safe questions and are now on to other questions, you can always come back to safe questions if necessary. The next time you're in a heated conversation and someone with an objection says something like, "Your price is too high!", "We don't want to do business with you anymore!", or "What's wrong with you?", go back to a safe question. In a calming tone, ask something like:

- What makes you say that?
- How can we earn back your trust?
- What would be most helpful to you?

You could even use tasteful humor to lighten things up and get back to a safe conversation, sometimes just by momentarily changing the direction it's going, until the tension is dispelled. It helps you keep your cool as you respond in a nondefensive way. This can actually save a relationship which could turn out to be of mutual benefit later.

No matter what the situation, when the conversation seems to be falling apart, always go back to a safe question. Remember, safe questions help the other person feel secure by affirming them, while observing their energy and pacing yourself accordingly. Safe questions create an environment for wonderful conversations. As Ralph Waldo Emerson said, "The only way to have a friend is to be a friend." Be a friend to others by sincerely asking safe questions.

Some Safe Questions Include:

- How are you doing?
- What's the best thing that happened to you today?
- What's going on in your world?
- What have you been up to lately?
- What have you been doing for fun?
- How is your family doing?
- Read any interesting books lately?
- Seen any interesting movies?
- What are the kids doing these days?
- Take any trips?
- How are the grandchildren?

—Chapter Five—

Closed Questions

Closed questions ask for true or false, yes or no, or multiple-choice-type brief answers. Closed questions, especially those that elicit one- or two-word responses, allow for the quick flow of ideas and can help speed up communication. While they're valuable for obtaining specific facts, if used exclusively, people may feel as though they're being interrogated. Some suggested beginnings for closed questions are: what, are, do, who, where, which, and how many. Some examples of closed questions include:

- Did you like dinner?
- Can we go out and play?
- Did you get the order?
- Which one do you want?
- How many times have you done that?
- Is this something you want to do now?

Unfortunately, many people know only how to ask closed questions, leaving them wondering what causes them to get very little feedback from others. If you use only closed questions, you may receive responses like, "What are you, an investigator or something?" If this happens, you need to go to a safe question to establish rapport. This type of reaction tells you that your skills need some fine-tuning. As you practice asking questions, you'll hear these types of comments from time to time. If you make a mistake, however, you can correct it.

As you continue to refine your questioning skills, you'll be even more observant that change is constant, both in the world and in you. Your insight about and compassion for others will increase and your horizons will expand as you embark on new adventures with renewed sparkle. You'll also find you're more keenly aware of, as well as discover the true meaning of, "response ability"—your ability to respond to other people's questions. You'll also notice *their* skill level as they question you, or fail to do so!

If a conversation is going on longer than you might like, lay a little groundwork perhaps responding, "I hear what you're saying," then make a signing off statement followed by a closed question: "I just have a couple more minutes before I have to leave. Is there a final point you'd like to share before I go?" This will enable you to gently indicate that your interest level may not be the same as it is for the person you're talking to. If you want to continue, ask an open-ended question, "Based on where you are in your career, what would give you the freedom you're looking for?" This can assist you in establishing rapport, enabling you to create a climate of acceptance—so you can move forward with the conversation. We'll explore open-ended questions in the next chapter.

Rapport Isn't Always Necessary!

There are times when rapport isn't necessary, when you may need just a couple of quick answers. They can be garnered with minimal effort by asking closed questions.

A great skill in asking questions is to know when to pace and lead. Pacing occurs when you match, or follow, the movement of the other person. It establishes an atmosphere that allows you to ask questions that help you gain knowledge you don't have. This is where closed questions can get you facts or input. It may also cause the other person to broaden his or her answers because of the respectful, kind manner in which you delivered the questions. For example, "Have you ever thought about how you can get out of the situation you're in? If I had some ideas to help you move out of it, would you want to know about them?"

Closed questions help you obtain information more expeditiously. Every day, most of us spend a lot of time asking and answering closed questions. As you develop your awareness of the nuances of asking questions, you'll choose your questions based on the situation. For example, you wouldn't ask your mother or father the kinds of questions you ask your closest friend. And asking your boss or senior manager one type of question could destroy your credibility. Asking someone on a different level who is knowledgeable could be a better choice. The more significant the relationship or desire for credibility the better placed the questions need to be. Remember, you only get one "free" question—then you need to create all further questions based on the other person's feedback to you. A free question helps you initiate the process.

You only get one free question. After that people generally know where you are going.

Learn by Doing

Now you may not be at ease asking uncomfortable questions. Especially in the beginning, you may feel all questions are uncomfortable. It's possible you may be playing it safe, are afraid of the responses you'll receive, or you're judging your skills as inferior. I appreciate those feelings. During the early part of practicing my own question-asking skills, I had people give me weird looks, turn around and walk away. However, by encouraging myself and doing what I feared, questions are now a part of my everyday life. You can have this skill too.

You can become more at ease with uncomfortable questions by *first* asking them of yourself. In the beginning it's not important to answer; just notice how it feels to ask.

The *next step* is then to notice how you feel when *you* sincerely respond to your *own* questions. Chances are, the response you give to a question you ask yourself will be similar to how someone may answer you.

The *third step* is to begin testing the waters; ask a question and watch what happens. Gradually you can experiment with a variety of questions so you can observe and learn from the responses of others.

Give yourself five to ten minutes a day to practice asking yourself questions. The better your self-esteem, the more willing you are to experiment. The worse your self-esteem, the more likely you are to stay in a cocoon and play it safe. Since self-esteem is the respect you feel for yourself, ask yourself, "Do I have enough self-esteem to do whatever it takes to leave the cocoon and turn into a beautiful butterfly?"

The person with the skill has the power.

Gapping Questions—*the Worst Case Scenario*

The worst thing that can happen is you will ask a gapping question—a pattern interrupt—and not connect with the person. Accept this as a possibility and you're on your way. You've probably already experienced this. Gapping can be observed verbally, nonverbally, and tactually. Verbal gapping occurs when someone comes back at you and says, "Well, not exactly." Or, "What I meant to say is...." Nonverbal gapping can show up in a look, taping fingers on a table, jiggling of a foot, and other ways.

Have you ever had a person just give you that look that seems to convey, "What are you talking about"? Their words don't say that, yet their behavior does. Tactual gapping involves touch. Have you ever been talking when someone suddenly touches your arm, breaking your concentration? How about when you were young? Did a parent ever kick you under the table for saying or doing something inappropriate? At that moment, you were gapping and your parent was tactually bringing it to your attention.

Have Fun Experimenting!

The skill and power of asking questions is to know when and what types of questions to ask. In a world where many people are sensitive to anything said and low trust is common, anyone who is sincere and has excellent questioning skills can make friends for life—anytime, anywhere.

One of the most helpful exercises you can do is write a list of typical situations you get into with various people on a daily basis. For example, consider your spouse, children, brothers and sisters, parents, boss, coworkers, strangers, and people you meet as you go about your daily routine. Develop a list of questions you can ask based on those typical situations.

I find it fun to visualize myself coming in contact with people whom I've allowed to intimidate me in the past. I see myself calmly going up to them and having an enjoyable conversation. How will you know what question to ask after you've walked up to someone? Notice the feelings you experience as you're approaching them and you'll sense the potential mood of the person. Take a deep breath and relax. As you calm down, your creative juices will flow, allowing your instinctive response to direct you on what question to ask. You'll find that your best questions can come from being focused on the other person and going with what your gut feeling tells you.

There is only one way to really know if anything I'm suggesting to you will work. Do it! As my father used to say, "Experience the experience of the experience!" This means go ahead and ask some questions and experience what it's like to do so. Have fun with it!

A person who's sincere and has excellent questioning skills can make friends for life—anywhere, anytime.

So in what situations do you need to use scripted closed questions? Let's test your skill. Your boss shows up surprisingly early in your area. You've wanted to ask his or her opinion on the report you gave last week. What questions could you ask as you walk by him or her in the hall? Or, you're on the phone with your spouse or a friend. You want to find out how receptive he or she would be to doing something together that neither of you has ever done before. How could you ask if they'd be willing to participate? Or, you find yourself in a situation where a friend has tipped you off to the fact that some people have an impression of you that you know isn't really true. Since you want to find out what they really think and feel about you and straighten out any misunderstandings, what question could you ask?

What did you come up with? Here are some closed questions that could be helpful for each situation. First, consider the situation with your boss walking by. You could say:

- Excuse me, Dave, could I have a moment to get your opinion on something?

- Susan, I need a moment of your time. Could you please help me?

Most people love to feel needed and like being asked to share their opinion.

Now, regarding approaching your spouse or a friend about doing something new together, you might ask:

- Would you be open to reading a book that I picked up yesterday? It's about learning how to _____ .

- If you had an opportunity to significantly increase your income without affecting your occupation, would that be of interest to you?

"Experience the experience of the experience!"
—William J. McGrane Jr.

By creating an element of adventure and a sense of curiosity, people, especially if they know you, are more likely to be open and trusting of you and willing to check out something with you that you're excited about.

Finally, let's consider the situation where some people apparently have an impression of you that isn't really true. You could ask:

- Tom, if I were to ask your opinion on how I come across to others, would you be willing to share it with me?

- I have an important question to ask. Would you be straight up with me?

A closed question can create a natural opening for additional questions to be asked, depending, of course, on how the person responds to your first question. One thing's for sure. In virtually every case, no matter what kind of questions you ask, doing so will lead to more interesting conversations than if you hadn't asked!

Think about all the questions you've always wanted to ask but, because you were afraid of the other person's response, you never did. There is definitely a time and place for questions and, for some, a degree of courage required. As you fine-tune your skills, the risk of offending others diminishes. When someone has the skill, they also have power to communicate more effectively. As you become more skilled at asking questions, you're on your way to some very intriguing as well as pivotal conversations.

Take several moments now to write some closed questions, just for the experience of doing it. You can analyze all you want; however, it's only when you take action that you can expand your skill of asking questions and, thus, expand your relationships. Now stop reading. Get a pen and a clean sheet of paper and create five to ten closed questions.

Here's a list of some suggested closed questions:

- Do you like your job?

- Will you be going to the conference next week?

- Do you have what you need to succeed?

- Isn't it...?

- Couldn't it...?

- Wouldn't it...?

- Don't you agree...?

- Haven't you found...?

- Do you know that...?

- Is it possible that...?

—Chapter Six—

Open-Ended Questions

O pen-ended questions are like essay test questions—they ask for more than a yes or no answer. They call for the individual to elaborate, inviting him or her to continue sharing when sensing your interest in hearing more. As a result, their energy increases. Open-ended questions can uncover a person's hot button, dream, or core criteria, and allow you to get better acquainted.

Some suggested beginnings for open-ended questions are: What, how, and in what way? Some examples of open-ended questions include:

- What's your opinion?

- What are we going to do about the situation with Bob?

- How shall we proceed?

- When would you like to talk next?

- How can we work this out so everyone is comfortable with your direction?

- In what way could we benefit if we bring in this other division?

Are you involved in any type of selling? While you may have said no, in reality, everyone sells. You sold your employer on hiring you. You are selling people on your philosophy of life by the way you behave. Have you ever encouraged anyone to go to a movie, ballgame, play, or anything else? You were selling them. If you're married, you sold your spouse on marrying you. If you have children, you're constantly selling to them and they often object! You sell to everyone and everyone is selling to you, so the real questions are: Do you realize you sell? Do you know what you're selling?

Discover Other People's Interests

Open-ended questions help us discover other people's interests so we can give them what they need, want, and value. A salesperson needs to know this in order to obtain the outcomes his or her clients want. By the way, children often recognize, at some level, that parents are doing and saying things for the parents' reasons, not the children's—so they refuse to buy, resulting in a lack of cooperation!

Go back into your personal history. Do you recall anyone asking you open-ended questions? Did anyone ever make you feel special by giving you their undivided attention? Did you feel comfortable enough to begin telling them more about yourself? Consider how your family, acquaintances, friends, teachers, spouse, boss, and co-workers know you. Some know you better than others. Why? What's the difference? Is it possible certain people have more of an interest in knowing you at a deeper level? At some point in each of these relationships, wouldn't you agree that a certain amount of open-ended questioning has occurred?

Open-ended questions help create an accepting atmosphere conducive to self-disclosure—sharing information about yourself that is normally held inside. Only personal knowledge shared that is new to the listener represents disclosure. Self-disclosure involves at least one other person and it helps people better relate, identify, and perceive. You're always disclosing by the way you walk, talk, dress, and act toward others, write, ask questions, and do other things. Virtually all of this is open to the public, except, of course, what you do inside your home. You can't help but self-disclose, at least to some degree. The more you share of yourself the more *you* know yourself.

The more vulnerable and open you are to others, the more apt they are to self-disclose to you. This enables you to create the connections you need to deepen your relationships for greater growth. However, it is necessary to have appropriate self-disclosure, based on the subject matter being discussed and the person with whom you're sharing it. The questions you ask are, themselves, a form of self-disclosure. You can comfortably ask only those types of questions that you've already asked yourself.

One of the most important immediate goals of asking questions is to learn more about yourself and others. However, you need to be open to discovering more about yourself. As you get to know and accept yourself more, you'll become increasingly open to asking questions and truly knowing and accepting others. You can only ask questions, know, and accept others to the degree that you know, accept, and ask questions of yourself.

The JoHari Window

The JoHari Window can assist you in being more open to self-disclosure as you get to know yourself and others better. It's a graphic model of interpersonal relationships, originally designed for Human Relations Training Laboratories by psychologists Joseph Luft and Harrington Ingham. It's a window through which you can give and receive information about yourself and others (see sample on next page). Observe how open-ended questions can fit into it.

The upper left is known as the Open windowpane while the upper right is the Blind window pane. The lower left is the Hidden windowpane and the lower right is the Unknown, or Unknown Potential, windowpane.

"Now how does this window illustrate how people choose to self-disclose?" you ask. As you'll discover, these panes, in reality, may not be evenly distributed or balanced. For example, you'll notice that you are more open with some people and situations than others. Your open pane is larger with your best friend than it would be with an acquaintance. Therefore, it is possible that the other three panes are smaller when you are with your best friend.

How would you really like to be with others?

Open (known to self and others)	Blind (known only to others)
Hidden (known only to self)	Unknown (known to nobody)

The Open Windowpane

The Open windowpane is the area known to both you and to others. It's the information, behaviors, attitudes, feelings, desires, motivations, and ideas that are public knowledge. This window pane varies in size depending on the situation and the people involved. According to Joseph Luft, "The smaller the open windowpane, the poorer the communication." The emotional depth of your communication depends on the degree to which you open yourself up to others and yourself. You can have meaningful communication only to the extent you know yourself and others—*to the degree your window is open.*

At one time, I wasn't very open with my father. I had mentally put him in a box and closed the lid on it. As I shared before, he sliced and diced people with his words, and I wanted to minimize his potential for attacking me. So I didn't allow myself to be vulnerable with him. Even so, he often directed a lot of harsh communication toward me. When I risked being more open and let him out of the box, I discovered his ever-evolving state of mind and behavior. He was continually growing, refining his knowledge and skills, and giving himself away to everyone he met.

As a result of my openness in sharing with him, I received much knowledge and mentoring, and learned various skills. These are treasured moments in my life where he and I, together, experienced the deep fulfillment of a father-son relationship, as well as the bonding of a mentor-mentee relationship. These moments have taught me to be as open as I possibly can to everyone, in all situations, because I don't know who will be my next pivotal teacher or when he or she might arrive. It could even be my two sons, John and Jay, or daughters, Laura and Heidi! Although, I have to admit, I learn from others all the time. My teachers are everywhere—and so are yours!

The Hidden Windowpane

The Hidden windowpane is known only to you, not others. It includes information that is both relevant and irrelevant to a conversation. There may always be portions of yourself that you never choose to disclose. Some information you choose to keep to yourself and some you don't—depending on its nature, the situation, and the people involved. You disclose to some people while not to others. In total, though, you can disclose most of who you are, much more than you may be doing. The goal is to disclose appropriately.

For example, say you're at a social event engaged in casual conversation with someone about your and their children and their activities. It would be inappropriate to all of a sudden say, "When I was fired from my job, I didn't know what I was going to do." This is inappropriate to mention in that arena where no information about job situations was being inquired about or exchanged. It would disrupt the flow of conversation. The firing would need to remain in the hidden pane. Have you ever been uncomfortable being with some of your friends, yet chose not to let them know that? The kindness factor undoubtedly entered into it. Some things are better left unsaid, examples of the hidden pane.

The Blind Windowpane

The Blind window pane indicates what is not known to you while it's known to others. It includes defenses, ticks, or habits you're not consciously aware of such as saying: "you know," "ah," and "I mean," instead of using the power of the PAUSE. The pause can be your most effective tool. Many people feel they need to fill all the silent spaces of a conversation with words; however, pauses give time for digestion of and reflection on what was just said. You'll notice skillful presenters and conversationalists use the pause. They appreciate the value of this brief silence.

Use the power of the pause.

When you pause and eliminate fluff from your sentences, people are more likely to hang onto every word you say. Have you ever noticed how some individuals are so interesting to listen to that you can't wait to hear what's coming next? You can discover who these skilled people are by observing the crowds around them.

The ideal outcome in the blind windowpane is for *self-discovery* to occur through asking questions and listening externally. It takes no skill and it's easy to tell people about their blind spots. However, the person with the skill will help an individual figure it out for him- or herself. When people discover for themselves that which has been blind to them, rather than just being told, they own what they've discovered. You can take whatever you want to tell someone and put it into a question like, "If you were not to go ahead with our plan, how could that affect you a year from now or possibly longer?"

Questions can help people discover solutions for themselves. For example, when I was in high school, my dad would give me five minutes to share information with an audience. My vocabulary at that time was more limited and different than my father's. So when I used a new word incorrectly Dad would give me one of those knowing looks and later scold me, "How could you use that word there? It doesn't fit!" Even so, this approach didn't serve me in adding words to my vocabulary. Later, as Dad's people skills improved, he would refrain from giving me knowing looks and, rather, would later ask, "Bill, were you uncomfortable with any of the words you used?" Or, "Bill, would you be interested in refining a word you used?" I then became very interested in knowing what the word was and began using my dictionary and thesaurus more often. I discovered my blind spots for myself and was able to make the words my own.

The Unknown Windowpane

The fourth and last pane is the Unknown one—things that are not known to you or anyone else. This is where our *potential* is hidden. Here there is often apprehension because of ambiguity and fear of the unknown. Everyone wants to know the specifics—the five easy steps, and please, oh please, list them sequentially! We live in an increasingly lazy, want-it-all-yesterday world. However life is a do-it-yourself proposition, filled with ambiguity.

There's no perfect roadmap for everyone, even one involving the asking of questions. No one knows exactly what each day will bring, from the moment they wake up to the moment they fall asleep. There are always surprises, the unexpected—some are painful and some are pleasurable. Do you have the skill to handle both and create your life the way you want it? Questions can help you and others discover a solution to any situation or issue, including longstanding challenges that have been shoved aside and even thought hopeless. You may be surprised! So, with this in mind, view life as a new adventure every day. Be open to whatever happens each day, without judging. Use your energy and creativity to be innovative, and be sure to enjoy the process.

When I was 17, I joined the NSA (National Speakers Association). During their national convention that year, I decided to interview the seasoned professionals. They and their world were unknown to me so I made a list of people to interview, created a script, and went searching for those I wanted to talk to. Since I was also unknown to them, I first gave them some self-disclosure. It went something like this: Hi, my name is Bill McGrane III. I'm 17 years old and I'm a new member of NSA. May I have ten minutes of your time to interview you, (name)? Most of them said yes, to which I responded, thank you.

Next, I asked each of them the following questions: What do you speak on and how long have you been a professional speaker? How did you get involved in the speaking profession? What do you like most about being a speaker? What do you like least about being a speaker? What impact has travel had on your life and your family? If you were to start over again, what would you do differently? If I were your son, just starting out in the speaking field, what suggestions would you have for me?

The power of those questions introduced me to many magnificent, caring, giving individuals. Their responses helped me put together my own philosophy of how and what I wanted to create in my personal and professional life.

Signals Alert Us as to Whether a Person Is Open to More Questions

As mentioned earlier, when you start asking questions you'll get signals that let you know if that person is open to your asking them more questions. How can you know what those signals are? Are you able to notice feeling answers versus thinking answers? When a person responds to your initial question, notice the words they choose. Brain hemispheres are set up to differentiate between thinking and feeling questions. Left-brain dominant people prefer to be asked thinking-type questions. Right-brain dominant people prefer feeling-type questions. Through practice, though, we can learn to differentiate between people's thinking or feeling answers. This enables us to choose between asking, thinking, and feeling questions.

Becoming a whole-brain questioner will provide the widest range of communication.

Everyone has a vocabulary that will give you an indication as to what's important to him or her. So, what if you find yourself in a conversation that seems to be going nowhere? All of a sudden, you observe that the person you just met has put his head down. His voice becomes quieter and his speech slows. He may even stop talking. It's clear he's experiencing some kind of feeling about something. If you're comfortable having a feeling conversation, you could ask him an open-ended question to learn more about his feelings like, "What are you feeling now?" or "What feelings are you experiencing?" or "What are you experiencing?" When someone is connecting with his or her feelings, it's important for you to help that person feel safe and comfortable enough to feel those feelings.

Some people don't believe it's acceptable to have feelings. They look for any distraction possible to disconnect from what they feel or to minimize their feelings. Ask yourself, "Who have been my role models in experiencing feelings?" Were you raised in a home where your feelings were acknowledged and respected; or were you shut down when you started sharing your feelings? The next time you go to a movie that brings a lot of people to tears, observe the group when the lights go up. Notice those who are willing to take time to process their feelings and those who are not. What clues do you give off when you are in those situations?

Remember, feelings undescribed will eventually be expressed or described at some time in some way. Are you describing them in such a way that you and others are energized or de-energized? Do you feel like you're a victim at the mercy of others and share from that stance; or do you take responsibility for your situation and your feelings about it? Moment by moment you decide, as do others, whether or not you'll share your feelings. When people feel there will be no negative consequences for letting you know what's true for them, they're more willing to be open with you.

Ask yourself, "What signals do I give off that make it easy or uncomfortable for people to disclose their feelings to me? Do I squirm and fidget, losing eye contact when someone shares his or her feelings? Or do I remain calm, focused on that person, and loving in attitude?" We can only be comfortable with others to the degree we are comfortable with ourselves!

Make it a habit to daily stretch your feelings comfort zone. Give yourself permission the next time you feel a tightening in your shoulders, stomach, or neck to ask yourself, "What am I uncomfortable with here?" Or, upon noting your calmness, ask "What is it about this situation that makes me feel so relaxed?"

By allowing yourself to feel, you put in motion the greater opportunity to know and accept your feelings. Once you do, you'll know that feelings are just feelings. They are a reflection of your perception of any given situation and aren't right or wrong, good or bad. They just are. Sometimes, upon expressing them, though, a misunderstanding can be cleared up and your feelings will often change in light of the new information.

As you become more comfortable with your own feelings, the stage is automatically set for you to be able to respond more appropriately to the feelings of others. You'll be able to notice someone thoughtfully asking questions, and how comfortable he is with himself. You'll notice how this allows him to get beyond his preoccupation with his own thoughts and feelings— so he can focus on the person in front of him.

You'll know you are present and focused on the other person when you have no distracting self-talk going on in your head—no preoccupation with what you or they will say next. You're able to be fully in the moment and observe what is going on, while not allowing your own ideas or feelings to capture your attention. You're aware of what's going on in your head, yet able to quiet those experiences and be present to another person as you generously give the gift of listening.

This can be challenging since most of us are constantly trying to fill our own needs and wants, while perhaps endeavoring to impose our values on others. Consequently, we can easily get consumed by our own agendas. When you find this happening, use an anchor statement that you say to yourself to relax and focus back on the other person. For example, you could tell yourself: Be present; I am now present to the moment; or, I now focus on the other person.

Another powerful tool is breathing. By slowly breathing in through your nose and out through your mouth, you can recalibrate your attention and focus it again on the other person. Do it now as you are working with this idea. Breathe in through your nose and slowly out through your mouth. This oxygenates your brain, adding vitality and greater responsiveness. When you breathe out, you, of course, release carbon dioxide. Do this two to three times. If you go too fast, you may become lightheaded. The key is to slow your pace so that when you're listening to others your breathing creates an atmosphere of relaxation for both of you.

To take this idea a step further, combine your breathing with your anchor affirmation. Say to yourself, "I am now calm and relaxed." Now breathe in through your nose and slowly breathe out through your mouth saying, "I am now calm and relaxed." This is a powerful tool for calming down. This would be a great statement to post where you'll see it frequently—on your computer, by your desk, or in your vehicle.

When you listen to someone who's experiencing or expressing their feelings, eliminate any verbal, nonverbal, or tactile communication that would break their flow of energy. For example, a simple sneeze or a question asked too quickly could be enough to detrimentally change their energy level. Keep in mind that windows open from the inside. If we try to open them from the outside, they tend to break! People can only be as open with you as they are with themselves. Respect where they are and invite them to grow.

Open-Ended Questions Also Involve Asking *Thinking* Questions

These are questions that engage the left hemisphere of the brain. Culturally, most of us have been brought up in environments that encourage these types of questions. We tend to be at ease with thinking questions because we are used to answering and asking them. One affirmation you may choose to say is, "I am a whole-brained person who's comfortable asking both thinking and feeling questions."

When you listen to someone, you'll get word indicators as to their preferences. People will say, "Last night I was *thinking* about," or "Did you *analyze* that situation?" or "How could we *validate* that this is true?" Thinking questions tend to put people into a thought process that can be either long or short. Have you ever asked someone a question you thought would get you a simple yes or no answer, yet they went on for several minutes? Your question was interpreted as open-ended. That person feels comfortable with you!

Open-ended questions evoke both left- and right-brain responses. Become a student of open-ended questions, and watch your conversational pleasure explode. Notice how willing people are to share with you their greatest pieces of wisdom—often harvested from years of exploration and experience. Get to know people at such a deep level that they'll always feel connected to you. Ask them questions like:

- Who has made the biggest impact on your life?

- If you had to do it over again, what would you do differently?

- Who was your first manager and what did you like most about them?

- In order for you to go ahead with this idea, what do you need to feel comfortable?

Be a wordsmith and create open-ended questions. Every time you finish a conversation with someone, they'll look forward to being with you again! Some suggested open-ended questions include:

- How did you get where you are today?

- Tell me about yourself?

- What do you do when...?

- How do you...?

- What do you know about...?

- What do you like best about...?

- What makes you most alive?

- When you're not working, how do you like to spend your time?

—*Chapter Seven*—

Interview Questions

The fourth level of questions is interview questions. They zero in on a particular area and are more in-depth. They allow you to get to know someone better, setting up an atmosphere where values emerge. They're more intellectual than feeling, and are used to determine if there's enough common ground to pursue the relationship. Another purpose of interview questions is to help you listen externally, so you can better design questions around what the person is saying, using their words. For example, ask broad questions like, "If you had a chance to...?"

Interview questions can enable the questioner to get the conversation going in the desired direction. They often emerge from safe or open-ended questions. As you listen externally and hear each response, you can then design questions based on what someone is sharing with you.

Have you ever had an interview for a new position or been approached by someone with an opportunity? How many questions did *you* ask? Did the person interviewing you ask all or the majority of the questions, or were you proactive in designing and asking your own questions? Would you agree that an interview in a situation like that has a dual purpose? The organization is observing you as a candidate for a position or role, and you are observing the organization as a potential employer or something you may want to become a part of.

My father created an interviewing process for the students he taught at the University of Cincinnati. He encouraged his students to interview at least twenty-five organizations before accepting a position. Dad received great feedback, both from students and potential employers. They found the interviews to be refreshing and unique because the students also asked questions of the interviewers. The information in this chapter could serve you either as a potential interviewer or interviewee.

Questions can show more about you than just telling people what you know.

There is certain up-front information it would be wise to acquire before participating in any interview. This includes answers to the following ten questions:

1. How large is the organization?

2. What are its assets?

3. How long has it been in business?

4. How diversified are its products and/or services?

5. What kind of reputation does it have locally, nationally, and/or internationally?

6. What kind of management/leadership philosophy does the company practice?

7. What is the nature of the company's business?

8. Is the company in a period of growth?

9. What are its prospects for growth?

10. What are the greatest challenges to the expansion of this organization?

When you ask interview questions it indicates your interest in learning more. Do you watch any television? Have you noticed over the years that the interview shows, for example, talk shows, investigative-type shows like *60 Minutes* and *20/20,* Sunday-morning political shows, and others like them are getting top ratings? Why? People are intrigued by other people's lives and beliefs, particularly well-known people or others who have achieved some degree of fame.

Notice how each host has his or her own style of asking interview questions. The interviewers have all created a unique niche because of the style of their questions and the format of their interviews. If you want to see the impact questions can have on a person's income take a look at the salaries these people receive—largely because of the questions they ask!

Could there be a correlation between your income and the questions you ask? Are you asking enough people enough questions?

When you watch TV or listen to radio talk shows, listen intently to the interview questions, the interviewer's tone of voice, the words chosen, when they ask their questions, and how they position their questions. Observe the nuances of their style, then notice the responses they receive. Also observe the display of any insensitivity. The best in the business create a safe space where interviewees know their comments are going to be listened to and respected. The best questions are seven words or less.

Some interviewers have made a name for themselves by being tough questioners. Who comes to mind as a model of this? What's their style of questioning? All types of questions have their place, and skilled interviewers know when and how to ask them. Sometimes the last-minute or spontaneous question can be the most powerful and informational.

The Columbo Close

Years back, a wonderful model of interviewing was used in the television detective show *Columbo*. He used surprise interview questions to catch the villain. I use the following question based on the Columbo close concept. At the last minute, as I'm departing, I turn and ask, "Oh, may I ask you one more question?" I then casually walk toward the person and ask a core-criteria question, getting to the bottom of things. Columbo was a master at pulling all of his questioning together. What style! What flare! If appropriate, you, too, may want to use this closing concept when you're asking interview questions.

Make asking questions a relaxed, playful event, and you'll find great pleasure in knowing more about what others are thinking— so you can better guide them to a mutually beneficial outcome. For example, let's say you were offering someone an opportunity of some sort and the person rejected it. Like Columbo then, why not close your interview by asking if you may ask one more question? If given the go-ahead, you could ask something like: "If not this, what?" or "If not now, when?"

Could there be a correlation between your income and the questions you ask? Are you asking enough people enough questions?

Be Curious!

A person with self-esteem has curiosity. When you have learned to take care of yourself, you naturally want to focus your energy on others. People who are self-centered have little interest in knowing anything from or about others. Conceit and arrogance limit people's willingness to get out of their own worlds long enough to discover something new, or even old, about others. How many people have you known who, because of their lack of curiosity, were bored and, unfortunately, broke off a business or personal relationship that had great potential? When you continually nurture your self-esteem, you'll be more willing to get out of your own world and explore the wonders available to you in others.

Seven Key Questions for an Interview

There are seven key questions you need to be able to answer about the other person, whether you're an interviewer or an interviewee:

1. Does the person know the respected men and women in his or her field? It helps for you, too, to be current on people in the know.

2. Is this individual credible? When someone asks a person for their input, credibility is key.

3. Is the person articulate? Knowing a lot is not enough. One needs to be able to get ideas across in such a way that people want to listen and hear them.

4. Does this individual listen externally? Credibility is immediately broken when a person shows he doesn't care to really listen to what's being said.

5. Does the person ask incisive questions that get to the heart of the matter and keep people's attention?

6. Does this individual convey a sense of purpose? When you feel that someone has a direction and is focused, you believe more of what they say.

7. Does the person create a climate of acceptance? People don't care how much you know until they know how much you care; they want to feel accepted and understood. We feel most relaxed when we're accepted.

Examples of Interview Questions

As an interviewer, be sure to include these three questions:

1. What is your background?

2. What are your skills?

3. What are your hobbies?

These questions are broad and will give you an insight into asking more questions based on the answers you receive. If you're being interviewed, be prepared to answer these kinds of questions.

When you're interviewing or being interviewed, you may want to consider asking some of the following thirty-five questions, some of which include additional related question(s). Of course, you'll need to place whatever ones you choose in appropriate order suitable to your needs—to obtain elegant, exquisite, and irresistible outcomes.

1. Would you tell me about yourself?

2. Would you tell me about your company?

3. What do you like best about your job?

4. What do you like least about your job?

5. Do you have a mentor? How does he or she affect you?

6. What are your best skills? How do they help you get the outcomes you want?

7. What does the good life mean to you?

8. How would you describe your career path from high school to the present time?

9. What are your top five priorities? How did you pick those five?

10. What is the latest date on which you have decided to retire? How did you decide?

11. What does success mean to you?

12. What is happiness for you?

13. What would you like to change? What makes you say that? What would changing that do for you?

14. What is your energy level like?

15. What does your exercise plan include? What is it doing for your body?

16. What are your company goals?

17. What are your personal dreams, goals, or objectives?

18. What serious issue has your company faced this year?

19. What type of vacations do you like to take?

20. How important is your health to you and what might you do to maintain it?

21. What community activities do you participate in?

22. What qualities do you like best in an employee?

23. What do you like best about yourself?

24. What would you like to look back on as your greatest accomplishment?

25. Have you planned the rest of your life? What's your plan?

26. Would you share a little about your family?

27. How many dead-end jobs are in the company? What makes them dead-end?

The following questions will help you discover prime movers—forward-moving people who have an affirming attitude.

28. Would you tell me a story about your life that shows how effective you are?

29. How much of your own money have you invested in your personal and professional development in the past twelve months and for what specific purposes?

30. How would you evaluate your effectiveness?

31. Where do you want to be positioned in the future in terms of your responsibilities and rewards?

32. How do you get acceptable support for the things you want to do?

33. What use are you making of your knowledge of yourself?

34. What is your attitude toward responsibilities, risks, and rewards?

35. What would you do if time and money were not an object?

All of your questions don't have to work or be on target to accomplish your objective. You may periodically have questions that will miss. However, the more you refine your skills, the greater the probability you'll connect. When I'm with someone, I want to feel a connection with that person. Can you accomplish this with everyone? For the most part, yes! However, there are some people where a connection may not be possible, at least not at this time. Be prepared for whatever you might receive, and don't take any rejections personally. Other people's behavior is always about them. It may reflect their reaction or response to what someone else says or does, or something in their surroundings; nonetheless, it's *still* about them. All of us get rejected at various times, kindly or unkindly, advertently or inadvertently, even if this may not appear to be true because of a particular image projected. We all reject others and things in our sorting out processes of making choices, consciously or otherwise. For example, we can only have lunch with so many people at a time and choose just so many cereals off the grocery shelf every time we go food shopping.

Be prepared for whatever you might receive, and don't take any rejections personally.

You may not always be aware of the impact your communication is having as you ask questions. There's the question and also the message behind the question, and that message is sometimes communicated more strongly than the words used. For example, consider the question, "I'm not defensive, are you?" The words say one thing, however, the message behind them in the actual defensiveness displayed says quite another. The words and message are incongruent and send mixed signals. Clarity is essential for the best outcomes. Lack of it on either end garbles the message.

An important part of observing the effectiveness a question has in drawing someone out is in how long it takes for them to process and respond to what they hear and understand. Some respond immediately, while others may need more time. Just because someone doesn't answer right away doesn't mean you haven't reached them. It may mean that the question you asked is something foreign to them and you need to clarify what you mean; they weren't paying enough attention; they require more time to process it; or something else. With self-esteem, your questions are more likely to cause a connection with people since you are more in touch, in tune, with yourself and, therefore, with them too. You'll be better able to recognize the time needed for a response, and be more comfortable with the moments of silence in between.

People have different processing times. Some may need ten or fifteen seconds before they can respond. If so, pause, refrain from completing their sentences for them, and once they've finished, allow five to ten seconds before you ask your next question or state whatever you're going to say next. This'll also help with pacing, thus creating rapport. Would you agree that many people are shut down in conversations simply because others don't allow them to finish sharing? Have you ever done that? Has it ever been done to you? Just do your best with this every day and watch your relationships blossom. People will give more in-depth responses when you give them the necessary time to find, discover, and process answers at their own rate.

Do you allow people to finish their own sentences?

Blend Talking and Listening

When you consider asking questions, decide if you're going to give people information or if you're only interested in hearing what they have to say. Learn to *blend* the two as appropriate. Have you ever had people ask you a question when all they really wanted to do was tell you their point of view? They just wanted to position themselves to say what they wanted to say. This is a manipulative rather than empathetic way to interview.

Have you ever had someone ask you a question, then when you answered it you realized they really weren't interested in hearing what you had to say? Didn't feel too good now, did it? You probably felt they didn't care about you. Check your intentions behind your questions. If you want to establish and maintain rapport, make sure you listen with undivided attention. If people get the signal that you're not interested in what they have to say, it will immediately break the rapport and energy.

Your Intentions Come Through

With all questions, especially interview questions, people can sense your intentions. They pick up on it through your body language, eye contact or lack of it, feelings, tone of voice, and the words you use. They sense if your walk and your talk are congruent, and whether or not you're really interested in them. Have you ever had someone ask you an in-depth question and, because of their behavior, got the feeling they were doing it just to be nice? Didn't that lower their creditability and sincerity in your eyes? Didn't it also affect the level of communication you were willing to give?

An Often Not-So-Honest Environment

In business today, or in any relationship, are you finding that people are not really saying what's on their minds? Do you find that the environment is often not conducive for them to feel comfortable sharing their points of view? They may say, "I'm not going to tell anyone what I think; I might lose my job. What if we downsize? I'm older than most of you." As a result, we're having to pay a big price in our government, institutions, and organizations. We may placate people and try to make them believe and feel something that isn't reality—to keep them in line and under our control. Yet, with the skill of interviewing questions and a sincerely concerned attitude, we could discover everyone's point of view and take it into consideration. We could then creatively find a point of view that could serve everyone, and possibly find solutions to some, perhaps, longstanding issues.

A Multi-Faceted Skill

Keep in mind there are many nuances to asking questions. You may be asking, "How do I keep it all straight? Are there any easy steps? Can you show me the specific sequence so I'll be successful?" I can only share with you what I have learned from what I've done, and that others have given me feedback that it's also worked for them. It's really quite simple. Do your homework ahead of time. Then, when you're with people, really *be* with them.

When I'm with someone, I put all of my homework away—all of my thinking and all structure aside. I go with the flow of the person in front of me. This means that when I'm with you, I'm not thinking about what question I'm going to ask next. I shut off my internal dialogue so my mind isn't spinning with mental chatter. I don't hear things like, "Is this a safe or interview question?" or "Am I in rapport with you?" or "Are you listening to me?" All of this is out of sight and out of mind. I'm not thinking about any of that. That was my homework—my preparation. It's now time to be present to the moment and focus on the person in front of me!

I learned this the hard way. When I was practicing these skills, I would try to remember all of my homework and people would undoubtedly walk away from me saying, "Boy, that guy's weird! There's definitely something wrong with him. Let's get out of here!" I was mentally "out to lunch," preoccupied with my own thoughts and feelings. I really wasn't being there for the other person.

When you're practicing these principles with someone, *be totally with that person*. Rather than thinking about the principles, let them comfortably nestle in your subconscious mind, where they belong, so they can emerge to serve you quietly as needed. Trust your inner wisdom and go with the flow. Follow the cues and clues of the person in front of you. After all, that person has the answers, even if he or she doesn't realize it. Listen externally and you'll have an adventure, and maybe even gain a new friend.

Now you may be asking, "Bill, how do I do my homework? Where do I begin? What's the best way to learn these principles?" The best way is *your* way. As you're incorporating the ideas in this book into your life, ask yourself this: "What's the easiest next step?" The answer is different for each of us. Commit to learning that easiest next step—then take it. Forget tackling the *big* item. Go for a guaranteed incremental success. Learn one new thing a day and, by the end of the year, you will have learned 365 new next steps.

Remember, it takes fifteen years to become an overnight success. I've been practicing these principles, on purpose, every day now for over thirty-seven years. Even so, I'll still continue to act as if I'm in kindergarten because they're part of a lifelong learning process. The outcomes are worth every second of effort expended in discovering, refining, and bringing myself and others into greater aliveness.

When I conduct seminars, the results of attendees who create wonderful outcomes are directly related to applying the skills I'm sharing with you now. Not only can these ideas help you improve your financial picture, they'll support you in acquiring something even greater—psychological income. You'll be equipped to create better relationships and have the satisfaction of knowing you've made more of a difference in other people's lives.

Now it's time to write down five to ten of your own interview questions. As you do, keep in mind that there may be some people in or coming into your life who you're going to interview in the near future. Maybe you're going to be in a meeting soon where you need to speak with your supervisor, manager, or leader, or you're going to make a presentation. Design some questions that may be useful to you now as well as in the future. Or, perhaps, there are questions developed by others in your line of business or work that you can use to be more successful in relating with others. Here are more suggested interview questions:

1. It sounds like you never get to.... Would that be something you'd be interested in?

2. Who do you call upon to help get you back up and going again when you're at your lowest point? What would be the reason to choose this person?

3. What are you going to do if you can't change the situation?

4. At this point in your life, what are you looking for?

5. What are you looking for in a business opportunity?

6. How do you feel about...?

7. What do you think about...?

8. As a result of what we've talked about, what seems to be the next best step for you?

9. Would option A or B give you more of what you want? What's your reasoning?

10. What's been the greatest challenge you've overcome so far? How did you overcome it?

—Chapter Eight—

Congruent Questions

Congruent questions get to the core, are sensitive and on-target. They are designed to cause great self-disclosure involving feelings and create harmony. Some suggested beginnings for congruent questions are:

- What would be needed for you to...?

- When did you decide...?

Congruent questions aren't always comfortable. However, when thoughtfully and skillfully asked, along with previously established rapport, trust, support, and sensitivity, an individual will generally continue to respond. The potential life-affecting reflection that a congruent question can encourage is a rare occurrence for most. If you have experienced such an exchange, you can clearly recall the words spoken, the time of day, the place, the person, and the outcome you received. This is not an everyday event. People who aren't yet in touch with their feelings and those who are just beginning to do so, especially men in certain cultures, tend to have the most difficulty with this level of questioning, as their feelings can seem ambiguous.

In order to effectively use congruent questions, you first need to be congruent with yourself, as well as with the person in front of you. Basically, you need to be in harmony—what you think, say, do, and feel are consistent. You also need to have the best interest and well-being of the other person in mind. When you're congruent, you deal directly with the feelings, thoughts, and reactions associated with any issue. It takes a lot of energy, undivided attention, and use of all of the skills discussed. Nevertheless, the outcomes are well worth your investment. Congruent questions can be life giving.

There are many people who ask congruent questions, even though they may not be interested in harmony. They don't care about the outcome, relationship, or the person in front of them. They may use a congruent question only to stir someone up or just to get some sort of response. Very often in these instances this manner of congruent questioning involves a lot of nervous laughing, which they would describe as humor.

People often use humor inappropriately—to release or cover up pressure, lack of self-esteem, or uncomfortable feelings. For example, people often use cynicism to mask related or unrelated animosity and distrust. This doesn't serve anyone. They may be laughing on the outside, while in emotional, physical, or spiritual pain, crying on the inside. Many people who endeavor to be funny while asking congruent questions find that the outcomes they receive aren't very satisfying. However, they're unaware of the gap they create which causes people to want to leave, physically, emotionally, or both. In an effort to retrieve the conversation and minimize the poor outcome their ill-placed humor caused, their response might be, "Oh, I was just joking."

This is ineffective communication. The more you truly care about others and the greater your skill, the deeper you can connect with them. They instinctively know your intentions are honorable, which is reflected by the sense of peace they feel with you, thus they're willing to go with the flow of your questions. As you ask questions with sensitivity and confidence, you'll be able to connect with virtually anyone and create elegant, exquisite, and irresistible outcomes.

Have you ever been asked a question, not fully appreciating its impact at that moment, or how it caused you to reach deep inside for the answer? Yet over time, as you digested the meaning of it all, you discovered a very powerful or unique message in your response. It may have even been life-changing. Congruent questions can have this kind of effect. The question is, do you know how to ask questions in an elegant, exquisite, and irresistible manner? My father shared with me that he liked to get into conversations and share ideas with people in such a way that they didn't even realize he was asking questions. He'd say, "I'm like a surgeon. I laser my questions so they go in and get out without blood."

An Effective Congruent Question Communicates Without Hurting Self-Esteem

We all have times in our lives when a congruent question is appropriate. For example, we all have boundaries that need to be respected. When someone steps over them and begins to abuse us verbally, mentally, or physically, it's time to ask a congruent question. Four favorites I've learned from my father are:

1. Do you feel better when you talk to me that way?

2. How is this choice moving you toward your highest and best?

3. Is that behavior helping you obtain the outcomes or results you want?

4. How can I support you in following through with your commitment?

Notice that with each of these congruent questions, I keep my and the other person's self-esteem intact. I use soft eyes, a soft voice, soft words, and a soft delivery. Everything I think, say, do, and feel is in harmony—congruent. There's no blame, judgment, shame, guilt, or punishment. I'm valuing myself enough to be congruent about questioning another person's behavior that's not serving me. Yet, I'm respectful that this person has some unreleased feelings around something that needed to be addressed. Remember, people only attempt to hurt others based on the degree *they* are hurting. So when someone invades your space or boundaries, attempting to inflict pain—*it's not about you!* It's this person's pain that he or she is attempting to release, and it's the only way the individual thinks they can do it at that time. This is an example of the McGranism, "Feelings undescribed when they need to be described will be expressed in some other way, at some other time."

When someone invades your space or boundaries, attempting to inflict pain—*it's not about you!*

When a person is expressing feelings there's *an impulse to reveal the feelings in any way possible—to eliminate the discomfort of having the feelings.* This could include yelling, hitting, total silence, ignoring, and addictions, plus all the violence we are presently experiencing in the world. Some violence, even though it may not appear to be, is a cry for love! When a person is acting the most unlovable is when they need love the most. On the other hand, describing feelings occurs when a person speaks and shares in words, as well as possible, what is going on inside. No words can totally or adequately describe a feeling. Traditionally, society has discouraged us, particularly men, from expressing our feelings. Unfortunately, there are major consequences for this behavior. If feelings are contained, they manifest later—internally or externally—in some other fashion, such as stress, disease, or violence.

Take charge of asking congruent questions when necessary. More than likely, immediate rapport with another will not be established in this type of situation. It could change the tone of what might have appeared to be a perfectly functioning relationship. However, the more you value the relationship, the more important it is for you to communicate congruently. As a result, you will have rapport with yourself because you are being congruent with yourself. You are the only one who is responsible for you, so create your life the way you want it and let others know your boundaries. You'll respect yourself more and so will others!

Some people attempt to hurt others based on the degree *they* are hurting.

Remember, you can only give what you have, nothing more. You first have to meet your own needs and take care of yourself before you can truly serve others. Then you can create a climate of acceptance where you can be totally present and focused on others by asking them questions, giving them an opportunity and permission to describe instead of just impulsively acting out their feelings. This allows them to discover new avenues of behaving which can give them better outcomes in their career or business relationships, and their lives in general. You cannot ease your pain by attempting to inflict pain on others—this only intensifies it. Remember, no one can hurt you without your permission.

Congruent questions have a place in your communication; however, they're not necessarily an everyday event. Your success with them is determined by how well you have established rapport and integrated the other four levels of questions: safe, closed, open-ended, and interviewing. When you use congruent questions, you need the other four levels of questioning to process the feelings, thoughts, and reactions of the person in front of you. When you practice asking questions, you can learn to ask in a way that becomes safe, secure, and as comfortable as possible for others, even though you may be asking congruent questions.

"Carefrontation" Versus Confrontation

After years of practicing and using congruent questions, I've created a system to deal with fragile situations that need to be addressed. Most people are familiar with the idea of being confronted, which as *Webster's Dictionary* defines it, is "to face, especially boldly or defiantly." However, I suggest you learn the alternative of "carefronting"—bringing up and discussing a delicate situation in *support* of a person or group. There are two types of carefrontation situations—spontaneous and planned.

In preparing to carefront, be very clear about your purpose in doing so. The following questions can help you obtain that clarity and get yourself out of the way, so you can pay undivided attention to the person being carefronted. Whenever possible, ask yourself these preliminary questions and consider these ideas before carefronting anyone:

1. What's the intent behind my proposed actions? Am I doing this for myself, for example, just to air my frustrations, or to support the other person?

2. Do I want to carefront or confront this person? Again, carefronting is being concerned enough to discuss a challenging subject in a kind manner. The outcome is to be self-discovery and growth for the person or persons being carefronted. Confronting is to face or meet a sensitive subject head-on, which has degrees of comparison and value judging, at the expense of destroying a person's or group's self-esteem. There's a tendency to be controlling in confronting—"You should, ought, or must do this or that." As a result of learning about carefronting, you may think you need to carefront somebody. However, all you really feel like doing is confronting and challenging them and getting

it over with. To successfully carefront, you need to truly care about others while exerting self-control; otherwise you might cause more harm than good. A cooling off period may be necessary before you speak with them again.

3. Do I want to "save" this person with what might just be a quick fix where they don't learn much, if anything, and maybe even create the same situation again? Or is my intention to help them discover something valuable for themselves and grow to the next level? Am I creating dependency or encouraging development?

4. Am I considered a credible source? If the person you're going to carefront doesn't trust you or believe you're reliable, he or she won't have confidence in you or listen to you. So going through an intermediary person as a bridge, one who has a better relationship with them, is an option, depending on the urgency of the matter. In any case, working to improve your relationship—healing or mending it—could pay off in the long-run.

5. Is this the moment to carefront or would it be better to do it later? Timing, delivery, and the surrounding climate need to be conducive to maximize the outcome of the carefrontation. For example, you would want some privacy from others when you'd carefront someone on a sensitive personal or business matter that only concerns them individually.

The Sequence of Carefronting

When you've worked through those five preliminary questions, you have yourself out of the way and you're ready to focus on the person to be carefronted. Here are ten nuances to the sequence of carefronting:

1. *Know your purpose*—Be very clear about the specific issue the carefrontee needs to discover. Know how this care-

fronting will serve the person (or group), and be helpful in getting them better outcomes.

2. *Let your heart be your guide and go with the flow*—The heart understands all things; it knows that it knows. When you truly listen to your heart, you're headed in the right direction.

3. *Create a climate of acceptance*—Give the person your wholehearted, focused attention with no judging, guilt, blame, or shame. Be relaxed, yet attentive, in your body language. Be aware of your facial expressions and eye contact. Soften your face, relaxing any facial tension. Have soft eyes, talk with a soft voice, use soft words.

4. *Build trust*—Remember, start where people are, not where you want them to be. Use all five levels of questions (safe, open-ended, closed, interview, and congruent) appropriately. What outcome is best for the other person? Does the person want or need to know what you know or is it just your agenda that you're promoting? Mentally file or store any information he or she shares, then only ask questions pertinent to this information at the appropriate time—when it feels like a natural fit.

5. *Listen externally*—Hear what the other person is saying and not saying. Are his or her words and behavior congruent? If you're unsure about anything, ask a question or questions until you get clarity.

6. *Be keenly aware of and tuned in to the other person*—Notice their tone of voice, posture, body language, facial expressions, patience level, timing, breathing, eye contact, listening style, and the values reflected in their words and actions. Also notice how they gain information: Is it by sight, hearing, or feelings? Do they say things like, "I see what you're saying"; "I hear what you're saying"; or "I'm angry/frustrated/excited"?

7. *Give your gift*—Share your intent, your purpose for being together. You may need to do this in a variety of ways. Speak from your heart and it's more likely your intent will be clearly sensed. Be sincere.

8. *Check that they received your gift and reaffirm your intent*—This involves listening externally. If someone becomes defensive or uncomfortable, allow that person to dump, letting them say what they need to say so they get it out of them. Let it flow; it's part of the process of reaching them. Never defend, justify, or explain. What they're experiencing may not be your experience at all. Everyone has their own perspective or vantage point, along with their own personal history that affects them in a myriad of ways.

9. *Pursue options to assist him or her to integrate new behavior, thoughts, or feelings*—Help the person discover alternatives that will give him or her the outcome he or she wants and values. Then be sure there's a commitment to act on his or her new findings. Encourage commitment if there's hesitancy. Remind the person of the outcome desired. Suggest simple, easy, success action steps.

10. *Acknowledge and appreciate*—Affirm the person for the choices he or she is making. Let him or her know that you'll be supportive as they move forward in their new behavior. Help them become aware that it's a lifelong learning process. Then remember to appreciate yourself for caring enough about another person to assist him or her in becoming the most he or she can be.

Dealing with Emotional Pain—*The Love Sandwich*

Many years ago, Brian, an old college friend, asked me out to lunch. This was normal behavior for us, and I was aware of a variety of activities that were going on in his life—including his upcoming wedding in two months. As we ate, Brian began sharing some of his challenges. Most troubling was that his relationship with his fiancée was not harmonious. Neither his friends nor his parents were supporting his decision to marry this woman. So I proceeded to ask him a few questions about the way he'd like things to be. Then I asked permission to share something with him and he said, "Go ahead."

I proceeded, "I care about you as a friend and want only the best for you. We have been friends for a long time and know each other well. Whatever I say to you is meant with only the greatest respect and love for your well-being."

I asked, "Brian, do you agree that you're experiencing peaks and valleys of pain in your present relationship?"

"Yes."

"Has the pain increased or decreased over the duration of your relationship?"

"It's increased."

"Brian, do you feel things will be easier once you're married?"

"No."

I then paused to double check my purpose in this conversation, asking myself, what is my intent in asking Brian these questions? I knew, for sure, it was to be a loving friend to him and help him get the outcomes he wanted in his life. So I decided to go ahead with a very congruent question that popped into my mind.

Since I knew Brian was a spiritual person, I asked, "Brian, is this relationship made of God?" Without hesitation he quickly said, "No, Bill, it's not. If it were, things would be harmonious and working. There would be no doubt or fear. My friends and family and her friends and family would all be supportive."

"So, what's next Brian?" I asked. "What do you feel is next?"

Remember, use only the person's words and never put your own words into someone else's mouth, so to speak. All I wanted to do was let Brian discover for himself that it's his life and he needed to create it the way he wanted it to be. I was there to be supportive of whatever decision he made.

Brian responded, "I need to call off the wedding, even though everything is set up. I need to get out of this relationship; it's not the best for me or her. Wow, what will everyone say? What are my friends going to think? I made a big decision and messed up!"

I then asked, "What's the worst thing that could happen and what's the best thing that could happen?"

Brian paused, then replied, "Well, I suppose I could be stoned, killed, disowned, left with no friends, and totally embarrassed. The best thing that could happen is that everyone would understand and I'd move forward with my life."

"So, what's your next step, Brian?"

He responded by giving me all the steps he was going to take to be congruent with himself, while maintaining his own as well as his fiancée's self-esteem. He'd first let her know that he was calling off the wedding and why, talk with his parents, let his friends and relatives know of his decision, and take all the other steps necessary to bring about closure.

Since Brian typically, in the past, delayed taking action, I asked, "Are you aware of the research that has found that if you don't take action on an idea within 24 hours, there's a 70 percent chance you won't act? If you don't take action within 48 hours, there's a 95 percent chance you won't act. How long will it be before you take action on the decisions you've just made?" This was a call for commitment, an agreement with himself, in this case, to act.

Brian said, "I'm taking action right now!" He began that very night, and by the end of the next day, he had completed all the major steps. I continued to support Brian and suggested he take some time to review his life and discover what he really wanted.

Years later, when we had lunch together, Brian said, "Bill, I wanted to get together with you to thank you, once again, for what you gave to me seven years ago. Without you saying what you said and asking me the questions you did, my life would be totally different today. I accepted your suggestion and went to your three-day seminar about attitude, interaction, and achievement. During that program, I wrote down all of the qualities I wanted in a wife and marriage relationship. Thirty days after that program I met my wife and, as you know, we now have a beautiful little girl."

This is applying the principle of the "love sandwich." Think of the bottom piece of bread as you saying something from your heart, complimenting or appreciating the person, like, "Our friendship really means a lot to me." Then the meat of the sandwich is the message you want to share, which you do with a congruent question. In Brian's previous situation, the meat was to suggest to him that he needed to reconsider marrying his fiancée. With the top piece of bread, you affirm the person again, which lets them know they are safe with and appreciated by you.

You may need to change the way you communicate and *be* with certain people in your life to get better outcomes. Brian and I, as friends, have made a decision to be congruent with each other and have an open, honest relationship. It takes compassion, courage, practice, and skill development to apply what you've just read. Be patient with yourself in the process. Remember, what's most important is that the other person knows you truly care about him or her as a person; this means more than words can say.

What if our questions aren't always on track when we have a carefrontation? Do the best you can to care about the other person while asking helpful, congruent questions, and be willing to lose the relationship. When you love someone enough to carefront them, you need to give them the space to decide how they will respond, including the possibility they'll never want to see or speak with you again. By not being attached to the outcome, it's easier to maintain your integrity with the communication, while still doing what's best for the other person! Their doing what's best for them *is* best for you, although this might not be immediately apparent.

The discomfort or pain involved can also pay dividends later on in that you'll be better prepared to handle other situations with more savvy. Your clarity in communication will increase and you'll eliminate certain challenges in relationships you may now have. As you continue carefronting, you'll probably notice that where you've employed these skills, your relationships are most likely much stronger than they were. When you carefront, you're going forward in improving your life as you support the other person in doing the same.

If, while carefronting, you find a person becomes uncomfortable or threatened by your questions or candidness, take a deep breath to relax and use the power of the *pause*. During this brief moment, go inside and ask yourself, "What's my intent?" If it's to love, care, and support, I encourage you to continue. With a soft voice say something like, "(Person's name), the only reason I'm sharing this with you is because I care about you. If I don't share what's going on inside of me, you may not discover the other choices you can make to get what you really, really want and don't have now. Would you prefer that I share with you what I'm experiencing or would you rather I keep it to myself?"

At this point, be prepared to respond to their request—either continue the conversation or *let it be*. Brian gave me permission to go on questioning him by responding to my heartfelt questions. I didn't tell him what to do and I didn't give him the gospel according to Bill McGrane or how I thought he needed to choose a mate. Instead, by asking questions and listening externally, I allowed him to tell me what his priorities were and I supported him through that process.

Put Your Carefronting Congruent Questioning Skills into Action

In what situation could you best apply the skills of carefronting with congruent questioning? It may be that someone isn't being sensitive to your needs, wants, and values, or perhaps someone is taking unfair advantage of you, putting you down, or being sarcastic. Write down five to ten congruent questions you could ask this person. You may have to work at it a little to design them, since most of us have been taught to be nice and quiet and not to stir things up. Now being nice is certainly a wonderful thing when it's good for everyone; however, allowing yourself to be taken unfair advantage of isn't good for anyone!

We've also been taught to pretend we're comfortable even if we're not. I know *I'm* not always comfortable. How about you? To grow and expand, choose to be comfortable about being uncomfortable. How can this be done? Put yourself in at least one uncomfortable situation every day, and you'll get used to it! So begin creating your own questions that you can ask in all kinds of situations. Remember, it's not important that the questions be perfect. They merely give you a benchmark of where you are here and now.

To grow and expand, choose to be comfortable about being uncomfortable. Put yourself in at least one uncomfortable situation every day, and you'll get used to it!

Now stop reading and write down five to ten congruent questions you can use during a carefrontation. Do you have any idea of the power of writing them down? When you write, you use all of your senses: sound, touch, sight, smell, taste, and your inspired sixth sense. You hear yourself internally constructing the questions, then experience the texture of the pen or pencil and paper. You see your question as you take a deep breath and swallow with delight, and possibly say out loud—"Ah, that's great!"

Experiment to learn if it makes a difference to you whether you type it into your computer or write it down. The more you practice writing or typing out questions for all kinds of situations, the sooner you can unlock your heart and have questions be a more natural part of your life. Even three-year-olds have it. And although their vocabulary is limited, they know the power of asking questions!

Life is a series of new beginnings.

Keep a list of questions and write down at least one new one a day. You won't be tested so just put on paper whatever comes up for you. Start the five levels of questions beginning with the easiest or safe questions, and work your way through the others. Next, design them so each has less then twenty well-chosen words. Then sharpen your skills and refine them further to have from seven to ten words. Begin noticing how many fluff words you're using—those that don't add any quality to your questions—and weed them out.

When you've done all this, you're ready for designer questions. Have a dictionary and thesaurus available. Begin the habit of looking up the meanings of words and finding synonyms to upgrade and refine your vocabulary, giving it more versatility. Ask yourself, "Is there another meaning for this word? Will people be clear about what I'm asking? Does this best convey the intended question? What are the nuances between synonyms? How can my questions bring people into aliveness and help them discover their own answers?"

The more you write your questions down (or type them) and practice asking them of yourself daily, the more effectively scripted you'll be, while still maintaining honor and flexibility. Now this doesn't mean you have every question in your head that you'll ever ask. The desired outcome here is not to memorize; it's to learn as many stem questions as possible. For example:

- Is it true that...?

- Do you agree that...?

- When was the last time you...?
- What needs to exist for...?
- Would you consider...?

Stem questions give you the freedom to add the specifics of the circumstances in the present moment.

Gradually, as you practice and refine your new skills with integrity, you'll discover more ways to put to use what you've learned. Then, all of a sudden, you'll be comfortable being uncomfortable and start receiving more of the outcomes you want. People will say, "You do that so easily. How did you get that way? I want some of what you have. How do you do that? You're a master."

Here's another McGranism that can serve you along your questioning life path: "Life is a series of new beginnings."

Some suggested congruent questions include:

1. If you had to do it over again, what would you do differently?

2. Will your choice to do something create a relationship you'll want to look back on?

3. What would need to exist for...?

4. If you don't do this, what will you do?

5. What was the turning point for...?

6. How would it be possible...?

7. If you did know the answer, what do you think it would be?

8. Do you have a better offer?

9. How can I earn your trust so we can...?

10. What's it costing you by not taking action?

—Chapter Nine—

Asking Questions Is Key to Persuasion

Using the sequence of persuasion can be a powerful tool in one-on-one, small group, or large audience presentations. It provides a simple and easy to remember structure in which to prepare and present your ideas. Use this information only in an integrative way—never to manipulate or take unfair advantage. When you act with self-esteem, you'll use this sequence to create only win/win outcomes.

Relax your audience. Make affirming comments about a couple of local landmarks. Self-disclose, sharing some things from your experience, allowing people to feel some relatability. Share about yourself and who you are. Possibly share a funny story. This can help others feel more comfortable with you and builds trust.

Ask five affirming questions, each of which can cause an easy YES response. Giving a yes is uplifting and can mentally draw the person(s) into your mutually beneficial way of thinking. It's affirming and often causes at least a hint of a smile. Know your audience so the questions you ask elicit their automatically saying yes, without even thinking. Ask short, easy questions that can build a favorable momentum of receptivity toward whatever it is you're sharing. Stem questions do the following:

a. Mentally engage others into conversation.

b. Orally cause them to respond.

c. Physically get them involved.

Here are several suggested stem question beginnings:
- Is it true...?
- Do you believe...?
- Would you agree...?
- Have you ever...?
- Is it important...?
- Do you think...?
- Would you like...?
- Is it reasonable...?
- Do you feel...?
- Are you aware...?
- Have you noticed...?
- Would you say...?
- Do you appreciate...?
- Are you interested...?
- Is it possible...?
- Are you open...?

Ask the final question—How many of you...? When presenting to a group and asking this last question, "How many of you...?" get them physically involved by raising your hand. This is to cause them to automatically raise *their* hand, as well, getting them actively involved in your message. Once they have raised their hands, wait a few seconds before you lower your hand; that's the signal to lower theirs. They are most open at this point so go immediately into your message.

Share your message. You no longer need to ask questions in the message. It's best to keep your points to three. Three key points are easy for people to follow and remember.

Lead them to take action. At the end of your message, make a suggestion. This is where you're persuading others to take action by using the following five key words as part of your stem questions: Based on..., may I suggest.... For example, *"Based on* what I'm sharing with you today, *may I suggest* you learn more about the sequence of persuasion."

Another example would be: *"Based on* your desire to accelerate your success, *may I suggest* that you... (sample this product, read this book, go to this seminar, or whatever is appropriate for you to suggest.)" This leaves them with an action step to take.

Applying the Sequence of Persuasion Principle

Let's say you want to persuade someone to do business with you. Following are two examples of how you can apply the five steps to the sequence of persuasion.

First Example: Group Presentation Using the Sequence of Persuasion

Step 1— Relax Your Audience

Thank you for inviting me to speak at your national convention. It's exciting to see so many of you eager to take your business to the next level. Three years ago I could hardly pay my bills and felt all kinds of stress and pressure because I couldn't see a way out of my circumstances.

I then decided to be more open-minded and trusting of a new way of thinking, feeling, and acting. After that, my life and career success turned around. The first year I earned more money than I had during the previous five! I am here to share with you how you, too, can move forward in your life and make your dreams a reality.

Step 2—*Ask Five Questions to Which You're Can Get Automatic or Spontaneous Yes Answers*

The audience would respond by saying yes to each of the following questions. For example:

1. Did you come here today looking for tools to increase your success?

2. Would you say you're eager to find the gem that could take you to your next level?

3. Have you considered that you need new ideas now to further your success?

4. Do you feel you would like to be more successful?

5. Is it important for you to accelerate your success?

Step 3—*Ask the Final Question—How Many of You...?*

On the last question ask—"How many of you...?" while remembering to raise your hand when asking this final question—leading them to raise theirs. Raise it all the way, with enthusiasm, as you finish the question. For example, "How many of you would like to know, now, what you can do to maximize your success today?" After your audience has raised their hands, lower yours, leading them to lower theirs. Then go immediately to Step 4.

Step 4—Share Your Message

Many of you have been on the journey of your success for years. I've found the following three actions made the biggest difference in my success and they can do the same for you too. (Expand on each point.)

1. Reflect more.

2. Risk more.

3. Create a legacy, something that grows.

Step 5—Lead Them to Take Action by Making a Suggestion—"Based on..., May I Suggest..."

"*Based on* what I've shared with you, *may I suggest* you do more of the following: create a legacy and watch what happens to your success!"

Second Example: One-on-One Presentation Using the Sequence of Persuasion

Step 1—Relax the Other Person

"Hello, Tom, it's really great you're here. What have you been up to since the last time we talked?"

Step 2—Ask Four Questions to Which You Can Get Yes Answers, Followed by One or More Core Criteria Questions

You can get answers that will tell you what they need to do in business, where they are now, and what their objectives are so you can meet their needs with your product, service, or income-generating idea. For example:

1. Is it true you've been looking for a way to increase your income?

2. Is it important for you to find an income source you believe in?

3. Have you found yourself looking for the right fit?

4. If you could find something that sounds good to you, would you want to know more?

5. What is it that you need most? For example, the client/prospect may respond: "I need more money, and I want to be able to spend more time with my family and travel."

Step 3—Get Them Physically Involved

Instead of asking the question, "How many of you...?" and raising your hand, engage the person by getting them physically involved. You can do this subtly by handing them a piece of paper, asking them to take notes, or suggesting they physically go with you somewhere to show them something by saying, "Let me show you something interesting on my laptop," or whatever the recommended lead-in statement might be.

Persuasion is most effective when it is done in sequence and with integrity.

Step 4—Share Your Message

"For years I was asking myself the same kind of questions you've been asking.

"When I found this company/organization, I stopped searching because it provided me with what I was looking for—a situation where I could increase my success."

Continue your message and give them at least three true things they just said they need most. For example...

1. Financial security and freedom—expand on how what you're sharing can help them achieve this.

2. Spend more time with the family—expand on how what you're sharing can help them do this.

3. Travel—expand on how what you're sharing can assist them in doing so.

Step 5—Lead Them to Take Action. Make a Suggestion Using—"Based on..., may I suggest..."

"*Based on* what I have shared with you today, you can have more financial security, personal freedom, spend more time with your family, and travel. *May I suggest* you fill out this order form, so we can get you your materials to get started right away (or whatever the next step is)."

The sequence of persuasion is something you can use every day. Like anything else, with practice, rehearsal, and drill, you can master these skills.

—Chapter Ten—

Developing the Art of Asking Questions

"So how do I develop the art of asking questions?" you may ask. Simple. As you practice asking questions, your skills will continually improve and you'll have made it an art. There's an art to selling, leading, teaching, dentistry, doctoring, building relationships, parenting, studying, being a friend, building a home, building a business, acting, and so forth. As with any art, there's a systematic application of knowledge that can be developed into a skill you can use to effect a desired outcome.

Observe anyone who has a well-developed skill, and you'll realize they didn't acquire it overnight. They went through a process of continuing development involving many incremental changes—a series of events that show continuous change over time or a series of actions or operations leading to growth. As something is practiced and becomes a skill, it can be turned into an art which then gives you the power to make a difference in your own life as well as in the lives of others.

Think about the professions that have a practice, such as doctors, dentists, lawyers, and therapists. These individuals have developed an art in their field; however, they continue to educate themselves and practice their skills, recognizing that there's always something new to learn and apply. View asking questions as your practice in an art which is forever evolving. There's no end to developing the art of asking questions—there are no final exams to pass, no diploma. However, there's always a reality report concerning your skill, and it's reflected in the outcome or result you receive every time you practice asking questions. As you develop the art of asking questions to affect yourself and others in positive ways, you'll constantly be refining and expanding your skills and enlivening your relationships.

There's a process to the art of asking questions that will unleash its power for you. It's simple. However, simplicity often requires discipline in order to discover it. This is, of course, where asking questions enters the scene. Your self-esteem and the respect and concern you have for the well-being and growth of others are key. Sometimes simplicity and familiarity hide important truths and, as a friend, it can be your job to take a fresh look at your relationships and help others find these truths for themselves.

Make asking questions a lifelong learning process. As soon as you feel you have it down pat, challenge yourself to learn more. Then you can be more sensitive and caring, be more present—in the moment—to each person and be genuinely interested in the one(s) in front of you. My father, who was a master teacher in the power of asking questions, used to say to me, "Bill, I'm in kindergarten. There is so much to learn about asking questions."

As I mentioned earlier, I observed him constantly refining his skills. Every day he gave himself away through the art of asking questions. You can do this with every phone call you make, with servers at restaurants, family, friends, and with those you meet throughout each day. Even on his deathbed Dad was asking the nurses and doctors questions about themselves to bring them into more aliveness. When you practice the art of asking questions, you, too, will be using your power to bring others into more aliveness.

Twelve Keys to Developing the Art of Asking Questions

There are basically twelve keys to developing the art of asking questions:

1. *Be careful not to distract people while you're asking them questions*—This includes not handing them water, tissues, patting them on the back, holding their hand, interrupting them, and so forth. The reason for this is you want the energy of their speech to flow. When someone is touched or handed something, it breaks up their energy flow or possibly their thought and feeling patterns. Once the process is complete, you can do all of the above, including hugging the person, if appropriate. This also holds true when you are with anyone who is exhibiting emotional pain.

2. *Observe the person's body language and intensity*—Be aware of how they are sitting or standing. Are they using an open or closed posture? What are their facial expressions? What is their tone of voice? What feelings do you hear in their voice that may not be in the words being spoken? Is their body tense or relaxed?

3. *Use your body language to give the other person permission to share with you openly and totally, without holding back*—Let the person ventilate his or her feelings. I call it the "upchuck" effect. In order for this flow to take place, avoid these four behaviors: a) never interrupt; b) never finish their sentences; c) never add anything; d) never defend, justify, or explain anything or yourself. Any of these four behaviors will immediately take the energy away from the individual and put the focus on you, stopping the flow. If that happens, it's very likely the person will choose not to continue in the same vein because they will feel, consciously or unconsciously, that you are not genuinely interested in or concerned about them.

4. *Use the power of the pause*—When the person is silent for a moment, hold off asking them a question. Pause for five to ten seconds to make sure they are finished with their thought or feeling. You can also use the pause when you are unsure of the next best question to ask.

5. *When you speak, soften your voice and use soft eyes and soft words*—The more intense the other person's voice, the softer yours needs to be. This helps create a climate of TUA, Total Unconditional Acceptance. It is also subtly giving the other person permission to describe his or her thoughts and feelings.

6. *Use the person's name before you say anything*— The most important sound to anyone is their name. Use their name often—it's music to their ears. Their name brings about peace and tranquility when used gently and lovingly.

7. *Watch the other person's eyes for a better understanding of what's going on inside them*—The eyes reveal encyclopedias of information. It's been said, "Our eyes are the windows of our soul." Aside from receiving a sense of the inner person, eyes help you recognize how he or she accesses information. Most of us access through one or two of three senses: visual, auditory, or feelings. If the eye movement is looking up, the person is visual. If the eye movement is from side to side, the person uses auditory accessing. If the eye movement is looking down to the right, the person accesses through their feelings.

8. *Listen, listen, listen…externally*—As mentioned earlier, only when you listen externally can you truly hear what the other person is saying. Active listening is loving. Give the person your undivided attention. Listening requires more concentration than talking, and it's the only way you can learn more about the other person.

9. *Ask questions based on the words, data, or information being shared with you*—This is where the skill of asking questions is involved. All five levels of questions can be used; the key word here is "appropriately." You may be sequential or go from a closed question to an interview question, to a safe question, to an open-ended question—the sequence doesn't matter as long as it is appropriate to the relationship you have with the person and the subject matter. What matters most is asking the best questions to help the person obtain the best outcome for him or her. (For example, if you just met someone, you may need to start with a safe question first.)

10. *Help the individual make an agreement on what he or she wants to do to obtain different outcomes from what they are now receiving*—Through asking questions, lead the person to agree to take at least one new action. And be sure to ask them *when* they'll take the action. Be specific. For example, "Mary, specifically, when will you speak to Mrs. Jones?" "What day in November? In the morning, afternoon, or evening?" If a person continues doing what they've always been doing, they'll continue getting what they've always been getting. It's unrealistic to keep doing the same things while expecting different results. Help them do something new that can give them the opportunity to obtain new results.

11. *Encourage feedback*—Have the person let you know that action has been taken. Again, do this by asking questions. For example, "John, how will I know you have talked to the Joneses?"

12. *The single most important ingredient in developing the art of asking questions is having self-esteem*—With self-esteem you can do it; you can create new outcomes and support others in doing the same.

To summarize the ideal elegant, exquisite, and irresistible outcome of asking questions, it's that the other person (or people) feels TUA—total unconditional acceptance from you. Sometimes, he or she may feel uncomfortable searching their soul for answers to your questions. That's okay; it's just part of the growth process. Nevertheless, when the conversation is over, they feel so affirmed and accepted that they may thank you—even if you challenged their behavior.

People are like bestselling books—just "shouting" to be read. However, most only ever have their table of contents read, if that. Take a sincere interest in other people, and they'll be more likely to gravitate toward you. Regularly focus on and care about others—by asking questions and listening closely to their responses. This can eliminate loneliness and futilely searching for people to bring into your life or business activities.

Continue developing the art of asking questions. You'll then have one of the quickest and best ways possible to create successful, fulfilling friendships, as well as love, and desired personal and professional outcomes.

Ask questions and listen—*then watch what happens to your success!*

Questions, Questions, Questions...

Below are lists of questions you can ask yourself and others. Use this to stimulate creating your own questions—*then watch your results soar!*

Questions to Ask Yourself

- How do I need to grow so I can get where I want to go?
- What do I really, really want?
- What's most important to me now?
- What makes me most alive?
- What do I need today?
- What do I want today?
- What do I value?
- What am I attracting into my life?
- Do I like what I am attracting in my life?
- Am I getting the outcomes I want?
- What worked today?
- What didn't work today?
- What can I do to improve my life?
- Will I forgive?
- Will I forgive the other person?
- Will I forgive myself?
- Will I ask the other person to forgive me?
- How am I being thankful?
- How am I being grateful?
- What's the lesson I can learn from this situation?
- What can I do to improve on...?
- What have I been avoiding doing that I need to do?
- What's the next step I can take?
- Who do I need to call?
- How can I reframe the situation?
- How can I focus on the solution?

- What solutions do I need now in my life?
- How can I make this win-win?
- How is my behavior affecting others?
- What would God want me to do?
- What would God want me to say?
- How is my thinking affecting my results?
- How are my feelings affecting my results?
- What do I need to do to improve my financial picture?
- How can I be more effective?
- What's working?
- What's not working?
- How can I be more loving?
- How can I be more responsible?
- How can I be more other-centered?
- How can I be of service?
- How can I be more alive?

Questions to Ask Others

- What is it you're looking for?
- What makes you say that?
- How did you arrive at that thinking?
- How did you arrive at that conclusion?
- How did you come to that decision?
- What if you could...?
- If you *did* know, what do you think the answer could be?
- When was the last time that...?
- If you could create it the way you want it, how would it be?
- What are you looking for at this point in your life?
- What is most important to you now?
- How would you...?
- How would you know you have it?
- What would need to exist...?

- How did you arrive at that feeling?
- How would you like it to be?
- What are you looking for at this point in your career?
- Would you like to have your own business?
- How would you know that you have what you really need and want?

Statements to Influence Others

- I can understand that, yet when I found..., I then came to a new understanding.
- I understand what you mean. In fact, I used to think/feel the same way. However, when I found....

When you share something or make a statement, follow it with a question. This is illustrated in the Sales/Career examples below:

Sales/Career

When someone objects to what you are offering, you could say the following:

- I can understand that.... You may not be interested. Yet when I found what they were offering was a new method never offered before and I could see and hear it was true, I then came to a new understanding that caused me to want to know more. What could I share with you so you can decide for yourself if what I found could be true for you too?
- I can understand what you mean, I used to think/feel the same way. However, when I found this company, their integrity, and what they offer, it changed the way I now look at them. What is it that you truly want?

Relationships/Family

When someone objects to what you're saying, ask the following questions:

- What do you need for me to be a great parent to you?
- What do I do or don't do that gets in the way of our relationship?
- I can understand that. You may think I'm saying the same thing I have always said. However, when you let me finish, you will hear I have changed. Would you allow me to finish please?
- How can we agree on the best way to communicate with each other?
- What do you need to be successful?
- How can I best support you?
- If you could do it over again, what would you do differently?
- What makes you most alive?
- What do you need from me at this point?
- When I found…. Does that make sense to you?

Keep in mind, you may need to vary the words you use and how you say it, so that over time people you are speaking with don't feel you are like a broken record.

Here Are Some Stem Beginnings You Can Use to Launch Questions

A stem question is the beginning of a question that you can use in a variety of situations. Stems can help you when you don't know where to go next in a conversation. Perhaps you've hit a dead spot and you need to re-energize the exchange by focusing more on the other person. Here are some examples:

- Is it true...?
- Do you believe...?
- Would you agree...?
- Have you ever...?
- Is it important...?
- Do you think...?

- Would you like...?
- Is it reasonable...?
- Do you feel...?
- Are you aware...?
- Have you noticed...?
- Would you say...?
- Do you appreciate...?
- Are you interested in...?
- Is it possible...?
- Are you open to...?
- What would need to exist...?
- What if you could...?
- When was the last time...?
- Could you get excited...?
- What would happen if...?
- If I could...?
- If you could...?
- Would you consider...?
- If you were given the tools to...?
- If I could help you get where you want to go, would you...?

Staging Questions that Allow You to Go Deeper

- What would cause you to...?
- If I were to...?
- Isn't it amazing...?
- When you...?
- However, if...?
- If you knew it could be true, then what...?
- That could be true, and what about...?
- If it could work, would you consider...?
- Does it make sense to you that...?
- What do you suppose that does...?
- What's it costing you by not taking action on...?

- Thank you for sharing. What makes you say...?
- How did you arrive at the conclusion that...?
- If you could do it differently, what would need to exist for you to...?
- If you were to do it over again, what would you do differently about...?
- What do I need to do to earn your business?
- What do I need to do to earn your trust?
- What's the reason you're doing what you're doing?
- What causes you to continue...when you know it is no longer working for you?
- What do you want to accomplish with...?
- What do you want to achieve by doing this?
- What is the bottom line of...?

A Selection of Feeling Words

Happy Words

aglow	enthralled	good	peaceful
alive	excited	grateful	pleasant
amused	exuberant	great	pleased
beautiful	fantastic	inspired	positive
blissful	feel good	joyful	relieved
brilliant	felicitous	jubilant	satisfied
bubbly	fine	lighthearted	smiley
calm	fired up	love	terrific
cheerful	fortunate	lovely	thankful
compassion	full of life	lucky	thrilled
content	gay spirits	marvelous	tranquil
delighted	giddy	memorable	trusted
ecstatic	glad	merry	turned on
elated	gleeful	motherly	uplifted
enjoyable	glorious	overjoyed	wonderful

Sad Words

angry	downcast	hurt	sober
apathetic	downhearted	lonely	somber
bad	downtrodden	lost	sorrowful
blue	drab	low	sorry
bummed out	dreary	low spirits	terrible
burdened	dull	melancholy	turned off
crushed	embarrassed	miserable	uneasy
deflated	emotional wreck	mistrustful	unhappy
dejected	feeling	moody	unloved
despairing	unwanted	morose	unpleasant
despondent	forlorn	mournful	unwanted
depressed	gloomy	negative	upset
disappointed	glum	painful	wistful
disenchanted	grave	pitiful	woeful
distressed	hate	plaintive	
disturbed	heavy-hearted	remorseful	
down	hopeless	self-pitying	

Angry Words

aggravated	disturbed	indignant	provoked
agitated	enraged	inflamed	rage
anguished	exasperated	infuriated	raving
annoyed	fed up	intense	rebellious
blustery	fierce	irate	revengeful
burned up	fiery	irked	riled
critical	frantic	irritated	seething
cross	frenzied	livid	sore
cutting	frustrated	mad	spiteful
disgruntled	furious	madness	stormy
disgusted	hateful	mean	temper
dismayed	hostile	miffed	ticked off
displeased	hot-tempered	ornery	troubled
distraught	in a stew	outraged	uncontrollable
distressed	incensed	perturbed	unrestrained

Confused Words

abashed	dismayed	jumbled	surprised
addled	disordered	left out	trapped
anxious	disorganized	lost	troubled
baffled	disoriented	mazed	uncertain
befuddled	distracted	mistaken	uncomfortable
bewildered	doubtful	misunderstood	uncomposed
bothered	embarrassed	mixed up	undecided
chaotic	flabbergasted	muddled	unsettled
confounded	flustered	nonplused	unsure
crazy	foggy	obscure	upset
dazed	forgetful	out-of-it	vague
delirious	frustrated	panicky	weak
depressed	helpless	perplexed	
deranged	helter skelter	puzzled	
disconcerted	hopeless	scatterbrained	

Scared Words

affrighted	distrustful	panic-stricken	timid
afraid	fearful	panicky	timorous
aghast	frightened	petrified	tormented
alarmed	harassed	rattled	tremulous
anxious	horrified	shaky	uneasy
appalled	insecure	shy	unpleasant
apprehensive	intimidated	spooked	unstrung
awed	jumpy	startled	worried
chicken	leery	stunned	
confused	lonely	terrified	
daunted	meek	terrorized	
displeasure	nervous	threatened	

Weak Words

burned out	helpless	mild	unable to cope
confused	ill	pale	unconvincing
deathly	impotent	passive	undernourished
deflated	inadequate	powerless	unfit
defective	incapable	puny	unhinged
defenseless	incompetent	quiet	unsound
deficient	inconsistent	retiring	unstable
delicate	ineffective	run-down	unsure
disabled	inferior	shaky	useless
dull	insecure	sickly	vulnerable
exhausted	irresolute	soft	wish-washy
exposed	lacking	spineless	wobbly
fading	laid low	stale	worn out
feeble	languid	stressed out	
fragile	lethargic	submissive	
frail	lifeless	subtle	
frustrated	lost	timid	
gently	meager	unable	

Strong Words

able	everlasting	intense	reliable
active	faithful	invincible	resistant
adequate	fierce	loud	robust
aggressive	firm	love	secure
angry	forceful	mean	solid
assured	formidable	mighty	stalwart
bold	full of spirit	muscular	staunch
brave	glorious	opinionated	stout
capable	happy to be	overwhelming	super
competent	hardy	penetrating	surviving
confident	hate	positive	vibrant
consistent	healthy	potent	violent
courageous	Herculean	powerful	well-being
determined	impregnable	productive	zealous
durable	independent	quick	
enduring	indestructible	rage	

"Take a sincere interest in other people, and they'll be more likely to gravitate toward you. Regularly focus on and care about them—by asking questions and listening closely to their responses...

Then watch what happens to your success!"

—Bill McGrane III

Who Is Bill McGrane III?

Bill McGrane is a recognized authority on peak performance, organizational turnaround, leadership, and personal development. He has served as an advisor to individuals, leaders, and corporations around the world, helping them attain greater levels of success.

Highly respected as one of the world's foremost experts on personal and professional advancement, Bill has become renowned as a consultant, seminar facilitator, speaker, and author. Achievers who are already at the apex of success in their field call upon Bill to be their strategic advisor when they seek to solve critical problems or conquer new arenas of achievement.

Bill's credentials include a business marketing degree from the University of Cincinnati, exclusive training in the Disney development methods, and diplomas and certifications from completing nearly 400 professional development seminars. He is also a past president of the Ohio Speakers Forum.

Bill currently serves as the president and director of McGrane Global Centers. You may visit him on the web at www.mcgrane.com. He and his wife, Linda, have four children and make their home in Union, Kentucky.

Notes

Notes